MUSLIM GIRL

A Coming of Age

Amani Al-Khatahtbeh

Simon & Schuster Paperbacks

NEW YORK LONDON TORONTO
SYDNEY NEW DELHI

My love letter to all the little girls
who ever cried in the dark

Simon & Schuster Paperbacks
An Imprint of Simon & Schuster, Inc.
1230 Avenue of the Americas
New York, NY 10020

First Simon & Schuster paperback edition September 2017

SIMON & SCHUSTER PAPERBACKS and colophon are registered
trademarks of Simon & Schuster, Inc.

For information about special discounts for bulk purchases,
please contact Simon & Schuster Special Sales at 1-866-506-1949
or business@simonandschuster.com

The Simon & Schuster Speakers Bureau can bring authors to your
live event. For more information or to book an event contact the
Simon & Schuster Speakers Bureau at 1-866-248-3049
or visit our website at www.simonspeakers.com.

Manufactured in the United States of America

3   5   7   9   10   8   6   4

Library of Congress Cataloging-in-Publication Data is available.

ISBN 978-1-5011-5950-3
ISBN 978-1-5011-5951-0 (pbk)
ISBN 978-1-5011-5952-7 (ebook)

Forgive him who wrongs you;
join him who cuts you off;
do good to him who does evil to you;
and speak the truth even if it be against yourself.

—Prophet Muhammad, peace be upon him

Introduction

"I'm kind of playing the game right now," I told Contessa Gayles in the bathroom of Muslim Girl's overpriced Williamsburg studio in Brooklyn, New York. I was staring at my reflection in our light-framed vanity mirror, doing the makeup routine that I've learned works best on film and that has become second nature over the past few months. Contessa's camera was rolling, getting some footage for the CNN interview we were about to shoot.

Muslim Girl blew up over the past year, for lack of better words. Our work to amplify Muslim women's voices in mainstream media reached worlds of new audiences. We were getting republication inquiries, media requests, and columns published in major outlets we only ever dreamed of, and our work was being profiled everywhere from *Teen Vogue* to the *New York Times*. In January 2016, we became the first Muslim company to land on *Forbes*'s "30 Under 30" list, and I became the first veiled Muslim woman to be recognized in the media category. And now here I was, carving my dark black liner around my eyes with precision, getting that cat eye as sharp as the shards of another glass ceiling we were about to break. Maybe.

Chimamanda Ngozi Adichie warned us of the dangers of the single story, and mine—as privileged and seemingly mediocre as it may appear to us Western Muslims, and as endlessly fascinating as it may seem to those looking in—carries the weight of a generation of little girls eagerly searching for a reflection of themselves in the world around them.

I'm perfectly aware of my role as the Token Muslim Girl these days. It's fulfilling to know that the opportunities created by Muslim Girl have come from exceptional hard work and sacrifice, but it's disheartening to think that it must be because they have become lucrative to somebody out there who's definitely not us. They call us "palatable," and indeed my story is much easier to swallow than that of Abeer Qassim Al-Janabi. She was fourteen years old when American soldiers in Iraq gang raped her girl-child body while holding her family hostage in another room, before executing all of them and setting the bottom half of little Abeer's body on fire. I can spend days talking about how 9/11 impacted us Muslim youth living in the West, but our experiences pale in comparison to the recipients of our country's resulting foreign policy in the Muslim world. Yet, the stark dichotomy of our experiences are only flip sides to the same coin: an illustration of how anti-Muslim bigotry takes shape on different walks of life in different ways. The relationship between them is politically intertwined. I see us—we, the Muslim citizens of the countries exporting these policies—as the gatekeepers to the rest of the Muslim community-at-large. We have a responsibility to use our privileges, resources, and every avenue at our disposal to assert a change that will ripple out and alter the course of history.

I'm not really sure I understood what was going on when 9/11 happened, but I was old enough to feel the world shift on its axis that day and change everything forever. I remember it so vividly because it was confusing and chaotic, and the first time since my grandfather from Jordan passed away that I was enveloped by sadness all around me, yet this time it applied to everyone. That day has become crystallized in my memory not just for how harrowingly scary it was—how we didn't know what would come after that—but also because I deeply believe that my generation of millennial Muslims has, whether we like it or not, come to be defined by it.

We have become commodified in every demeaning way: Our bodies have become political targets in the service of returning America to the imaginary greatness it once enjoyed, which I can only assume was during the days of outright racial comfort and superiority of white people; at the same time, our bodies have been reprinted, sold, contorted to fit the only cool narrative society can accept, sold to us Muslim women in a way that makes us eagerly jump to celebrate the shattering of another glass ceiling.

I still remember hearing the story of Cennet Doganay—the French schoolgirl who shaved her head in 2004 in protest of France's new law banning Islamic headscarves from school—when I was in middle school. I watched a story of her on the news, a rebellious breath of fresh air amid all the headlines pounding me with horrible messages about what Muslim women stood for, and to my twelve-year-old self, it was like hearing that there was life out there. There were little girls who felt just as attacked and disrespected by their societies as I did, and this one was talking back. I wondered if I would ever have the same courage as her.

Abed Ayoub, legal director of the American-Arab Anti-Discrimination Committee, issued a statement in the winter of 2015, almost immediately after Donald Trump's call for a ban on Muslim immigration, stating that levels of Islamophobia at that time were the worst they had witnessed since immediately after 9/11. My heart hurt. I could not imagine a generation of little girls living through a Trump era—the terrifying possibility of a Trump generation—and enduring the same unsettlement that my friends and I did growing up, not just from navigating their own identities, but their surroundings as well. Enough is enough. The cycle needs to stop. In this case, it's less of a cycle and more of an uphill battle in which we toil. We're climbing toward the light with exceptional weight on our backs, digging our heels into the dirt of the past to gain our way to the top, only to slip—no, be completely knocked down—by an uncontrollable, newly emerging force that causes us to tumble all the way back to where we started, much to the jeers and cheers and additional trips of the bystanders around us. Everyone can see it happen, and complacency is a killer.

The best I can possibly do is speak on my own behalf, to be brutally true to my own lived experience, and share with you a snapshot of a walk of life that I believe has been shared by many of my brothers and sisters wandering the same familiar corridors of our English-speaking diaspora, never cultured enough for home and never American enough to truly belong.

I think we've become starved for people to actually listen to us. We've become so desperate to hear our own voices above all the white noise that we have willfully compromised and repackaged our narratives to make them palatable—to make them commercial and catchy, to make them headline-worthy, to sell a story that you will find deserving of your attention. We call it playing the game, because you consuming some semblance of our truth is better than you consuming whatever else is out there, conjured by someone else on our behalf. But that's not good enough anymore.

Chapter 1

The only time I ever cried during an interview was when I was asked to recall my memory of 9/11. Was it for *International Business Times*? The *Guardian*? I can hardly remember anymore. But, surprisingly, I had never been asked that question before, and it caught me so off guard that when I started describing the vivid image seared into my memory, the tears began to fall.

On September 11, 2001, Bowne-Munro Elementary School in East Brunswick, New Jersey, planned to hold its annual Yearbook Photo Day. We were all dressed up and excited for an excuse to leave our classrooms, go outside, and spend the day on our grassy soccer field, against whatever backdrop they had for us that year. There was an electric energy of anticipation when we got to school. Everyone was wearing their best clothes; the boys wore new sneakers and the girls had their hair plaited in cute updos, or their smiles beamed from between bouncing curls. My hair was always frustratingly thick and slightly unruly, but at least Mama tried to brush it straight for me that day, my uneven curtain of bangs resting just above my eyes. I always felt my best on Yearbook Day, if only because Mama was eager to get a new set of photos of me to add to her collection. She took pride in displaying what turned out to be a chronological evolution of my awkward haircuts over the years, in pretty frames among porcelain figurines in the heavy cherrywood cabinet that was only accessible in the dining room on special occasions.

Mama loved Yearbook Day. She had just bought me a new outfit. I was wearing a stiff pair of jeans and a blue shirt—I hated the color pink when I was a little girl and rebelled against expected "girliness" by always opting for blue and green, which is fascinating considering nearly everything I own is pink now—with a black vest over it. I finished the look by slathering on my favorite Bonne Bell Dr Pepper Lip Smacker. I was probably wearing a pair of dress shoes that I couldn't wait to show off. And I remember it was really warm and sunny outside.

From the earliest moments of our first period, however, something was weird. Actually, a lot of things were weird. First of all, it was eerily quiet in our school. The TVs in all of the classrooms, which were usually on the district's cable channel of PowerPoint slide announcements to the background tune of elevator music, were turned off. That morning, the principal didn't deliver our usual morning announcements over the PA system, either. Then, soon enough, we were told by our teachers, almost inconsequentially, that Yearbook Day was canceled. They told us pesticide was sprayed on the fields that morning so we couldn't go outside. I remember feeling confused and a little disappointed, but everyone else just accepted that we would take our pictures another day, so I did, too.

Our math teacher cried so much throughout the morning that some of us thought that someone in her family had died. I remember the class trying to make her feel better while faculty passed through the halls or popped in every now and then in a state of disarray.

"It's okay, Ms. Brady," we said to her when she was hunched over at her desk, her eyes red from the tears, her face contorted like she was hanging on by a thread that could break at any moment. "It's going to be okay!" we cheerfully encouraged her. That only made her cry even more.

Our young fourth-grade minds were not much alarmed by these events, nor did we really think to string them together. How could we? How could we have possibly imagined what was waiting for us?

Our school day finally ended with an unscheduled early dismissal, much to our delight. Somehow, our parents were already informed of this, because when I ran out of school, my mom, who was routinely late to pick me up, was on time and waiting for me. I ran up to the car and Mama leaned over the passenger seat to unlock the door for me from the inside. I opened the door and didn't even have time to climb into the seat before she said, "Amani, something happened today."

"What's up?" I asked, getting in and closing the door beside me.

"You know the Twin Towers?" she asked.

"No—" I responded, confused.

"You know those two really tall buildings that are next to each other in New York? That we were looking at and talking about how huge they were when Dad took us for a drive in the city?"

"Yes," I said, remembering.

"Okay, well, there's been a crash, and they're not there anymore."

"They're not there anymore?!" I asked, trying to understand. "Like, at all?"

"No, honey. They're not there anymore. Two planes crashed into them."

"What? There was an accident? Is everyone okay?" I asked naively.

"Someone drove the planes into them," my mom said, but I still was not processing what had just happened. For the rest of our five-minute car ride home, I kept repeating the same questions, not sure how someone could intentionally fly a plane full of people into a skyscraper full of people, nor that those two towers in the opening credits of my parents' favorite television show, *Friends*, could possibly cease to exist. They weren't there anymore?

When I walked into our home, my family was in the living room, their eyes glued to the television screen. My dad was standing beside the TV and my mother joined him. My baby brothers, Ameer and Faris, then three and four years old, respectively, were in the family room, watching *SpongeBob SquarePants*. My grandmother and Auntie Ebtisam were sitting on the long couch in the back of the room, reacting in Arabic. They were visiting from Jordan and living with us for one year at the time, enjoying their first trip to the United States. My twenty-three-year-old aunt had her elbows up in the air, her fingers at work twisting her waist-length black hair, usually hidden beneath a veil, into one tight strand that she distractedly wrapped around the outside of her ear, which was a habit of hers. They couldn't believe what had happened. "I had just taken them there a couple of days ago," my dad, or Baba as we usually call him, told me. "They looked up at the towers through the sunroof of our car in wonder." Now, suddenly, they weren't there anymore.

But, here, on our TV, there was an image of the Twin Towers with clouds of black smoke coming out of them. I was trying to understand how they got like that, trying to imagine how this could have possibly resulted from a plane crash—and then it happened. The news channel looped the footage—a scene that would continue to loop in my mind's eye, surface in my everyday, for the rest of my life—of two planes crashing into the sides of the towers. My eyes saw it. I was suddenly a witness to an evil that I was not even able to grasp, exposed to a tragedy that I only had the capacity to feel but not comprehend. Whenever the footage appeared in the broadcast, everyone in the room fell silent again, in a trance, probably not far from my own elementary struggle to make sense of what I was seeing.

And then, Baba said something that I didn't understand at the time, but that alerted me to the impact of the day's events beyond two beautiful towers—and, as I later would learn, thousands of people—not being there anymore.

"This is a horrible thing that happened," he told his mother. "And they're going to blame us. And it's going to get much worse."

"Sorry," I told the journalist. She paused to give me a moment to clear my voice, and I hoped to God she didn't think I was faking it—feigning emotion for some type of dramatic impact, or to prove my patriotism.

I hope she knows my pain is genuine, I thought. *I hope she doesn't doubt that a Muslim American can be this impacted by 9/11, too.* The truth is that 9/11 never ended for us.

Elementary school was a very difficult period in my formative years concerning the development of my self-esteem and self-identity as a Muslim girl. By the time I finished elementary school, the U.S. was already involved in the Iraq and Afghanistan wars. The feelings of vulnerability and lack of protection were only second to those that I experienced in middle school, where the early teen years got really brutal. But, I think for many of us, elementary school creates the most sensitive impression of where we stand relative to other people and our status relative to the world around us. That's when the bullying started.

It was that same year that I heard my first racial slur. By then I had already become a class target, so the epithet only intensified my sunken self-esteem that always forced me to bite my tongue, not talk back, not stand up for myself for fear of the bullying getting worse. By fifth grade, every social interaction was distinctly marked with the preceding thought, *Dear God, please don't let them put me down.* And then the first time my heritage was held against me as an insult marked the end of the days that I innocently took pride in my culture as a source of joy and the subject of class celebrations during Culture Day, naive to the implications of race and history. It made me realize that my brown eyes and dark hair and tan skin made me feel more than just ugly compared to the other girls.

It happened in math class. It was audible to our classroom table of four or five other students, who would witness and compound my humiliation. It was a student with black skin who said it, who was always eager to make fun of other people so he wouldn't get made fun of himself. It was a phrase that would resurface ringing in my ears with every photo and every scrap of footage coming out of the Middle East for a long time.

"Your people throw rocks at tanks!"

I could hear other students gasp. One Jewish classmate burst out laughing. My people. Throw rocks. At tanks? And in a few moments, as the blood rushed to my cheeks, I was awash with the realization that this insult was different. This one didn't sting like the comments that I smelled or that I was ugly or fat. Suddenly, I belonged to a people, and that people was something I should be ashamed of. Shame. I didn't know why I felt ashamed, and I wasn't sure exactly what he was referring to or why it was so bad. But I did recognize that it was different. And I did feel that it hurt. And so I told my teacher.

The student got sent to the principal's office, and the principal ended up suspending him. Upon receiving the news, my other classmates shamed me even more for telling on him. And thus began this weird dynamic of getting victimized and then either silencing myself or getting victimized a second time if I talked back. When I went home that day and told my dad, he was sad and angry for me, but then he waved those feelings away with a smile.

"That's something you should be proud of, Baba," he told me, in our living room covered in tapestries and Middle Eastern upholsteries. "Your people throw rocks at *tanks*."

My family wasn't exceptionally devout, but we were practicing Muslims. While I resented not being able to wear shorts in middle school because my dad thought they were immodest, I am now so grateful for having grown up within the fold of Islam—not only because Islam did, inevitably, evolve into a backbone and an identity for me, but also because had it not been instilled in me at an early age, I'm not sure I would have had the strength or courage to find it myself after Islamophobia hijacked my life.

Baba is an immigrant from Jordan. He came to America when he was twenty-six, thanks to an opportunity granted to him through the sheer luck of a visa lottery. He arrived with only a suitcase and $300 in his pocket, two-thirds of which was scammed out of him by the time he left the airport. He hustled in New York City to survive, working in convenience stores and staying in someone's rat-infested basement for free. When he was driving me home to Brooklyn this summer, after I returned from a trip with Microsoft to Egypt, we passed by his old dwelling, on Thompson Street in Manhattan, and he excitedly pointed it out to me.

While he didn't practice it as religiously as I think he wished he did, my dad always tried to teach us about Islam whenever he could. He would use the time during our car rides to tell me stories about the prophets or share morals from the parables. It was during those rides that he helped me memorize the last three chapters of the Qur'an, which I still repeat three times every morning to seek protection from the evil eye—a curse Muslims believe will cause misfortune—and I feel compelled to do this now more than ever. More than anything, he instilled in me the unshakable belief that the right intentions were more important than absolutely anything—and that if I stuck to my moral compass, I should trust that God will always see me through. Always.

Mama is a refugee from Palestine. Her own mother is a survivor of the Deir Yassin massacre in 1948. Deir Yassin was one of the first villages to be pillaged by incoming European militias, and those militias used the violence they carried out there as a threat to the rest of the Palestinians on the land: *If you don't get out, the same thing will happen to you.* Later on, when I researched Deir Yassin's history in high school, I would learn that my grandmother had survived purely by fate. The remaining villagers were piled into two buses: The one that my grandmother boarded was driven to the banks of the Jordan River, which she crossed with her family's gold—which would later be used to situate her family in Amman—hidden in a sash tied around her little six-year-old belly. The other bus was driven to the heart of Jerusalem, where its passengers were killed by the city's new inhabitants. I'm not sure how old I was when I came to understand the bloody history of our family, but my grandmother's story always led my mind wandering toward a little girl who shone like a phoenix, rising from the ashes.

My mother's family came to the United States when she was a child. She had a Farrah Fawcett haircut in high school and hung out on the track after school, and she took great joy in listening to the jams of her beloved '80s. She saved up money at her banking job to buy a bright silver Porsche with leopard-print lining that she was especially fond of, which my dad, her then-fiancé, crashed during his first drive. Her mother's strength was passed down to her in the form of steely resolve. Mama has always fiercely fought for me and my brothers, much like a lioness protecting her cubs; we were especially grateful for her protectiveness later on in our childhood. I still remember the year that literally every student in my class took turns making fun of me and calling me horrible names, even in front of a teacher who did nothing to rectify the situation. When I went to my guidance counselor, I was told that I must be the problem, and I should change myself to make them stop making fun of me. Upon hearing this, my mother called the guidance office, demanded to speak to the stupid counselor who had given her daughter such reckless advice, and threatened to sue her and the entire school district for victim-blaming an eleven-year-old. I was promptly called down to the guidance office the next day and issued a formal apology.

After 9/11, it was like a curtain had been pulled back on my family, casting them into the spotlight, and revealing to them a world that seemed to have always been festering behind a thin veil. My parents had to navigate this new territory leading a young and vulnerable family, while they themselves were being targeted. For most of my life, my dad has run his own electronics business, through which he sold video games, music, and toys. Immediately after 9/11, he feared for our existence in the United States. At the time, we had a store in an indoor flea market in our town, which was only open on the weekends and where he would work for a good eight years. He imagined the possibility of being unjustly interrogated by authorities or losing his business, or being arrested simply for his faith. The fear of attacks was palpable: His brother in Jordan urged him to consider moving our family "back home," out of his own concern that we would be targeted or killed. He told my dad, "Imagine how easy it would be for someone to come to your store and shoot you and your family point-blank. You have to leave."

The flea market became a microcosm of what was happening to our nation on a larger scale. My dad explicitly remembers the dramatic shift in language in the news: He watched networks quickly transition from covering an abstract entity called Al Qaeda throughout the '90s in a region that average Americans basically understood to be the Middle East, to employing sweeping language that implicated Muslims and the Islamic religion as a whole—no longer focusing on political disputes, but instead feverishly seeking to relate terrorist acts to the Qur'an and amplifying connections between the Muslim identity and violence. The change in rhetoric, he recalls, suddenly made it acceptable for other people to attack us with the expectation that they would be absolved of accountability. My family was placed in a position of extreme vulnerability and exposure, being attacked and alienated solely because of our religion.

One of the employees of another toy store in the flea market slashed all four of my mother's tires. This act of violence is still, all these years later, stuck in my parents' memories from that time. They could feel that it was only an extension of the type of violence people around us wished to impose on us, and it was one that was blatantly hateful, inconvenient, and costly. When my father went to the owner of the toy store to inform him of his employee's actions, the owner turned aggressive against my father.

"What? Are you THREATENING ME?" he angrily demanded of my big brown dad. "Do you want to BOMB ME?" he said. Later, instead of questioning the employee who had slashed our tires, the police who arrived would instead question my father regarding accusations that he wanted to bomb the toy store. The police were used like a weapon against us, as they had been for people of color for a long time. Becoming the scapegoat meant that anyone could hold your identity against you at their will. It became a wound that people could prod and poke to try to bend us at their pleasure.

The other vendors launched a petition addressed to the flea market management, in which they demanded that all Muslim vendors and their businesses be evicted. This, of course, empowered other vendors to increase their harassment of my family. I still remember "the Jewelry Lady" from across the aisle walking into our store and openly insulting my father, in front of me and his customers, while wildly waving the petition in her hands. It was painful to watch. I felt so sorry and confused about why my dad had to suffer, and I truly thought the Jewelry Lady was evil for hating us for our religion. I didn't understand how anyone could be that mean for no reason. As all of this was happening, I felt like the entire world hated me and hated us for who we were, and, damn, that was a heavy feeling for a child. I guiltily asked myself why God had chosen to make me be born Muslim when I could have just been born Christian in America and had my life be so much easier.

Our beautiful house in the calm New Jersey suburbs was egged, water-ballooned, and TP-ed. I remember the appearance and smell of rotting eggs. The dozens of colorful and broken latex balloons that surrounded our home would have looked pretty and festive if I hadn't been aware of the hateful sentiment that delivered them there. My mom was sitting under one of the windows in the living room with one of my baby brothers in her arms when an egg flew in and landed on her head, almost hitting her child. I remember this was the only thing she kept repeating when she found the teens who did it: "You could have hurt my baby. I don't care about the house, but you almost hurt my child. That's all I care about."

My Jordanian aunt and grandmother were scared that they wouldn't be able to return home, or that they would be arrested and accused of something horrific. One day, they were in the public restrooms at the flea market, performing ablutions to prepare for prayer. Lots of Muslims have known the awkward experience of getting caught with their foot in the sink. When other people walked into the restrooms and saw my family washing themselves, they crowded around my aunt and grandmother like they were freak shows and started calling them horrible names. My relatives didn't understand much English, but it was easy for them to understand the spite, hate, and anger in their tormentors' voices.

My aunt and grandmother's relative obliviousness to the happenings around them due to the cultural and lingual barriers became a strange outlet for me as I renegotiated the new climate I was navigating. My aunt and grandmother didn't know much beyond the fact that right here, right now, they were being hated for their religion, but there wasn't really anything they could do about it. They continued living their lives as they always had, while I was trying to survive unbearable judgment that I attempted to cope with in small ways. At the age of ten, I already knew that I shouldn't compromise who I was and that these moments called for resolve, but of course I searched for opportunities to avoid public scrutiny, judgment, or insult. Once, I remember my grandmother visited an accessories store in the flea market and purchased a white scarf with red hearts and English text on it that she didn't understand. When she put it on, to my horror, it said I HEART JESUS! I was terrified at what people would think, and ran to my dad to make her take it off.

"So? That's great!" he said. "We love Jesus, too. People should know that. And now she's wearing it on her head."

My father had this uncanny ability to shield me from my own negative thoughts, or those new internalized feelings of inferiority and embarrassment. He could take anything I was enduring and turn it into something noble or empowering. My aunt placed me in a similar situation that summer, when we joined my dad at his business location on the boardwalk at the beach. I spent most of the summers throughout my childhood with my father on the Jersey Shore, when he would stay there for weeks at a time to run his store, and I grew to take great pride in being a Jersey girl who slept just fine with sand in her bed. That year, my dad's landlord got us season passes to the Splash Zone Water Park across from our store, and I would go there every single day. The rest of the family would join us on some days, when my mom wasn't busy running the other store in East Brunswick, and on one of these occasions we decided that the entire family would spend a day at Splash Zone.

I almost had a heart attack when my aunt decided to join me for the raft ride, fully clothed, from head to toe, in headscarf, metallic silver button-down shirt, and black slacks. She stood in line with me at the very top of the slide, coolly looking out from behind her black sunglasses, among all the white families in their drenched swimsuits, making us the center of attention. Everyone was staring at us. I could not understand why she had to put us in that position, and I was so embarrassed that I couldn't wait to jump on the raft, rush down the slide, and get out of there.

When I went back to my dad's store, wrapped in a towel, wet hair falling in strands on my face, I was quick to unload on him what had just happened.

"Baba!" I said, pointing to the topmost slide at Splash Zone across the way, which could be seen from anywhere on the boardwalk. "Do you see that ride up there? The tallest ride at the water park? Auntie Ebtisam came with me, and she was wearing ALL HER CLOTHES, and it was so EMBARRASSING! Everyone was staring at us!" I told him.

"Wow, good for her!" my dad said. "She should be able to enjoy the ride just like anyone else. That took a lot of guts, didn't it?"

I was in the sixth grade when I first made the decision to lie about my religion. It happened one sunny afternoon on our yellow school bus, heading home from another exhausting day of middle school in which I constantly tried to blend away my differences and fit in, only to inevitably capture the attention of bullies in my classes, and even ones I didn't know in the halls. I would get taunted for being a "monster" as I walked to class in between periods, and all I ever wanted to do was disappear. I was sitting next to my "bus partner," Jesse, who was this Italian kid with nerdy glasses—a signifier at our school that made him slightly uncool, too, and thus gave us something in common—with a gorgeous thick shock of brown curls on his head. He was in my Italian class, and would be my classmate for the seven years I studied the language throughout school. The next time I saw him after we graduated was a couple of years later, in college, when he was a barista at Starbucks with a bunch of hickeys on his neck. It's always nice when the nerds get happy endings.

On this bus ride, we were sitting in the awkward silence familiar to those of us banished to the outskirts of social life, when Jesse broke it: "Hey, what religion are you?" he asked. Crap. I felt a wave of panic wash over me. That conversation probably lasted only fifteen seconds, but to my eleven- or twelve-year-old lost and insecure self, it triggered a repetitive loop right before my eyes of newsreel after newsreel featuring brown men who looked like my father in orange jumpsuits and women who looked nothing like me talking about what my identity represented. It was agonizing.

I didn't wear a headscarf at the time, so I had the chance to hide behind being uncovered. It was a distinctly different moment from my first day wearing a headscarf to school two years later, when I had a breakdown walking to class in the morning and seriously considered ripping the scarf off my head before walking through the school doors. But in that moment, in sixth grade, my frizzy hair catching the sun beaming in through the school bus window next to me, I had the chance to conceal myself within the veil of anonymity, ambiguity.

Finally, after what seemed like light-years of my guffaws and hesitation, I made a fateful decision that I would recall for thousands of moments after that. "Oh, I don't know," I replied. "Something Mediterranean, I forget."

I didn't realize it at the time, but that decision would become a pivotal moment in my journey. While maybe counterintuitively I thought it would offer me some relief—a small break from the exhaustion of being a Muslim in today's society, some protection from the constant barrage of judgments, stereotypes, and attacks raining down on me from the media and my surroundings—what it did instead was cause a sense of even more palpable shame to wash over me. I was perfectly entitled to hide. Even in Islam, God permits us to renounce our religion if we are being persecuted and under threat of danger. But despite knowing this, I think what I felt at the time was the supreme unease that I had just done something against my nature. I submitted.

It's funny, because that's how Western media wants to perceive us, right? Submissive. Girls hidden behind veils who are only told what to do, who only have the mind to either follow a male family member or outrageously commit to violence as our only animalistic form of expression. And yet, what is it exactly that Western society wants us to do when it imposes an impossible pressure on us to bend, conform, assimilate, submit? When French laws supposedly aim to "liberate" Muslim women from the compulsion of wearing religious garments by ironically forbidding them to wear religious garments, and then fining all Muslim women who dare appear in the public sphere while refusing to abide by such outrageous rules upon their agency, what is Western society trying to do but make us submit? When trolls leave comments on MuslimGirl .com threatening us, telling us to shut up and accept the Western violence inflicted upon us because at least it's not the otherwise somehow different violence that we would be met with in Muslim countries, what do they hope we will do but submit? When we are ridiculed and targeted for covering our bodies in the face of the hypersexualization of patriarchal Western society that demands we, as women, take our garments off—that is more comfortable with a pair of naked breasts than covered hair—what does Western society want from us but our submission?

We are not submissive. To the contrary, every step we take in our non-Muslim home countries, in spite of pressure, threats, judgments, and even laws, is a reluctant act of defiance. The Arabic word *islam* means submission—in our religion it means submission to God and God alone. You want us to submit. Submitting is not in our nature.

The shame I felt was two-pronged: First, I felt bad about myself, as might be expected given the societal pressure for Muslim girls to view themselves as inferior; second, I felt bad about my decision, which, though I had made it for the sake of survival, I saw as a lack of courage, integrity, and strength. Of course, I know now that I was only a child, and that that was an undue burden to place on myself, but what could I do? That's how society trained me and inevitably caged me in.

All my life I've been conditioned to feel that I'm "less than." It's hard to explain, but I know my sisters of color understand this weird feeling that sticks to your bones so early and so discreetly that it requires evolving some superhuman level of self-awareness to even notice it.[1] W. E. B. Du Bois described such confines in the context of the black community thusly:

1 W. E. B. Du Bois, *The Souls of Black Folk,* Chicago: A.C. McClurg & Co. [Cambridge]: University Press John Wilson and Son, Cambridge, U.S.A., 1903; Bartleby.com, 1999.

It is a peculiar sensation, this double-consciousness, this sense of always looking at one's self through the eyes of others, of measuring one's soul by the tape of a world that looks on in amused contempt and pity.

In many ways, this phenomenon can apply to both black and, more recently, non-black Muslims post-9/11 as well. Being indoctrinated early on into a society seemingly at war with Islam, I quickly became afflicted by this condition, marked by a feeling of severe inferiority compared to my peers. This isn't some WebMD diagnosis based on a bullet-point list of symptoms: The effects of this illness vary widely and, to be frank, the greatest symptom may be that we have possibly spent most of our lives searching for a WebMD of this nature, that affirms this phenomenon we have been feeling, that echoes our symptoms and their effects right back at us. That's probably how MuslimGirl.com came to exist: the WebMD of patriarchy and Islamophobia, all wrapped up in one and sealed with a media-friendly pretty hot-pink bow.

That inferiority complex really seized me by the throat for most of my upbringing. It wasn't just that I struggled to break out of the mental limitation of how far I could go, but the feeling even surfaced in little everyday concessions like letting someone else take the last seat because I was second-rate and thus not worthy of sitting in it. Or letting kids cut me in the lunch line in the cafeteria, not just because I didn't feel I deserved to speak up, but also because they were loud and cocky and I was crippled by the fear of the ridicule I'd suffer if I did speak up and say, *Hello, I'm here. I am a person, too.*

In fifth grade, we had a science project called Project Earth, in which we collated 1,000 pages of assignments we did throughout the year into one big binder to submit for a final grade. It was the biggest project any of our nine- and ten-year-old selves had ever done. Of course, it was out of 1,000 points, and the lucky few fifth graders who scored 1,000 out of 1,000—if there were any—were spoken of throughout the halls like urban legends for years after they left for middle school. But there was more: The kids who scored the coveted 100 percent were given the authority to decide the order that our classmates would be launching the makeshift rockets we built in science class for the school-wide outdoor watching party at the end of the year. Every year, the entire elementary school poured onto the playground for the day, faculty et al, and we got to watch the fifth graders launch their pretty, handmade, and hand-painted rockets one by one. Sometimes they shot into neighbors' properties and were gone forever, other times there was failure to launch, and the rest of the time we would run to find where the beautiful creations had landed, yards away. But each year, it was our great send-off for the fifth graders, much to the delight of the rest of the school.

Lo and behold, I and two other students opened our graded binders to be greeted by the mythical "1,000" in red Sharpie with a circle around it. In the weeks that followed, we would meet up and sort the deck of index cards with our classmates' names written on them, deciding the order in which everyone would launch the rockets that we had excitedly been working on for months.

This is where that inferiority complex kicked in. We had decided that the three of us would go closer to the beginning so we wouldn't have to wait so long. I offered to go second. Now, why did I choose No. 2 instead of No. 1? It might be easy to hypothesize why. Maybe I was too nervous to be the first to go. Maybe someone else needed to warm up the audience before my turn. Maybe the thought of being the first to go was a lot of pressure, what with the chance of my rocket not launching. But I posit that my offer to go second was an intentional repression of my inner eagerness, the dulling of a girl of color's ambition, and a manifestation of the way I viewed myself. Something inside me told me that first place was not an option for me. It was reserved for somebody else. It was like it was some sort of expectation ingrained in me that second was the highest I could go. There had to be someone before me, someone above me.

For the first rocket launch, one of the other students selected a girl in our class named Roxanne. She was a beautiful girl, somehow always with sun-kissed beachy hair, blue eyes like the ocean, and perfectly tanned skin—yes, even at ten years old. She somehow possessed this supernatural confidence that made her the coolest girl in our class every year. She was my first best friend in school, and our moms would bring us together for countless pool parties and movie dates throughout our childhood. Until, in typical schoolgirl fashion, I somehow became shunned and the outcast among the rest of the girls in my grade, and she replaced me with a cooler companion. She was the same girl who, only a couple of years earlier, in third grade, had gone up and down our morning line as we were waiting for the bell to ring our school day into session. She stared into the faces of each one of our classmates, going down the line, saying, "No, no, no, no . . ." until she landed on me: "Yes! You have it!" I wasn't sure whether to be excited or scared, so I asked her what it was that I had, and she responded, "You have a unibrow." That was the first time I was introduced to that undesirable feature that I unknowingly possessed, and I went home that day crying to my mom that I had a unibrow. Thus began

24

my lifelong insecurity with my body hair. It's cool, though: Bushy brows are a thing now, apparently.

I think my science teacher, Mrs. Rabii, sensed that I was holding myself back. When she came to check on the completion of the index card deck the day before Rocket Day, she asked, "Who's going first?" saw Roxanne's name, and asked if none of us wanted to be first instead. I met her with silence. But that was the first moment that I ever imagined myself being first; the fact that it was offered to me like it was just as much of a right due to me as it was my peers opened my mind to picturing myself first. Being second was a cap I had placed on myself that I had never encountered, identified, or been aware of before. I stayed silent in that moment, but after I went home, I couldn't stop thinking about it.

I want to be first, I told myself. That was it—I had to be first. I planned to wake up early the next morning so that I could get to class first and change the order of the index cards. Even though I set my alarm, I couldn't sleep that night. I lay wide awake, in a sweat, watching the clock creep closer and closer to Rocket Day. When it hit an early-morning hour that was acceptable to appear in school, I booked it. But, when I got there, the stack of index cards was already in the hands of the other 1,000-point students, who were looking over the arrangement one more time before we went out onto the playground. Mrs. Rabii came over and noticed some type of unsettled nerve in me, because she turned and, almost nonchalantly, asked me, "Do you want to be first?"

"Yes," I said. And without hesitation, without so much as looking up, she grabbed my index card, moved it to the front of the stack, closed the box on the cards, and that was that.

That's all it took. I needed to decide that I wanted to be first. That I could be first. That I, too, deserved to be first.

Chapter 2

When I enrolled in an all-girls public school in Jordan, I didn't expect to memorize the picture frames on the principal's walls after my umpteenth trip to her office because our class leader kept looking for any reason to give the American girl a demerit. This time, it was because I had decided to wear the metallic olive-green jacket that I had just gotten for Eid, our Islamic holiday, over my lame schoolgirl uniform. Our uniforms were usually cut the same—the summer we got to Jordan, I had mine tailored and asked the man altering it to give it a dropped waist, to make it *somewhat* unique—with a short green pleated skirt flirting above its owner's pair of blue jeans, or black pants, or maybe even white or navy slacks. On the day that I wore a magenta button-down shirt on top of the uniform, with the top button strategically undone to show a hint of the silver heart necklace I was wearing around my neck, I learned that jewelry wasn't allowed either. I had gotten a hang of the strict dress code by the time Valentine's Day rolled around, when I took off the bright red scarf I was wearing right before I got to school in the morning and shoved it in my bag as I walked into class so I wouldn't get in trouble. *Red? On Valentine's Day? Do you have a lover or something?*

"Amani, you know you can't wear bright colors on top of your uniform," the principal gently told me, as if my American sensibilities had to be tiptoed around. I could tell she was annoyed seeing me in her office every week and did her best to dismiss the other girls picking on me. "It's against the rules."

The uniforms were the least difficult part of school for me to get accustomed to. When my father decided to uproot our entire family and move us back to his home country, he thought that enrolling us in an English-curriculum American school in Amman would defeat the purpose. This was an opportunity for me and my little brothers to not only meet our extended family, but also become acquainted with our culture, language, and country of origin. What better immersion than to, you know, throw me into eighth-grade-level Arabic textbooks when I could barely understand the conversational vocab my dad spoke to us at home? At least my little brothers were at an age where it was still somewhat acceptable to learn the Arabic alphabet.

My father had finally decided to make the move because he wanted to take some of the pressure of Islamophobia off of us. He actually did it. Minorities commonly joke about leaving the country if a certain leader is elected or if an event takes place that could prove adverse to their respective communities, and it wasn't until years later that I realized that's exactly what we ended up doing. My father didn't want us to be ostracized, to have to endure the extreme judgments of our peers or bear the horrible weight of being vilified by our society. He heeded his brother's concerns about falling victim to violence and refused to place us in harm's way. He hoped that by taking us to Jordan, he would provide us with a valuable experience that would contextualize our lives in the greater world around us.

You'd think that given everything I was going through in school and how hard it was for me to fit in, I would have welcomed the move with open arms, but it was a difficult one. The night before our flight, my dad found me lying on my stomach on the hardwood floor of my newly empty computer room, clutching a pillow and bawling my eyes out. "Baba, it's going to be okay," he told me in the dark, with only the secondary light of the kitchen streaming in and outlining his silhouette. "It's going to be like a new adventure." My dad gave me the expectation that the society I'd be entering was ultra-conservative, and so, on our way to the airport, I broke off the press-on nails I wore to impress the girls at my school and tried my best to prepare for an experience where I could not imagine what to expect.

Our arrival in Amman was like the grand return of a lost child home, one that demanded the utmost celebration. As soon as we landed, we were swept up by the overwhelming tides of family. In the airport, my brothers and I greeted and shook hands with people with unfamiliar faces but easily recognizable warmth—smiles we had never met, speaking a language we could barely understand, but knew we were related to somehow. We met one of our dad's two older brothers for the first time, Ummo Khalil, whom we always heard about but could never place. We all squeezed into Ummo Khalil's small van as though it were a clown car, and off we went to his house, where dozens more family members were waiting for us. The air around us smelled of gasoline and wrestled with the aromas of shawarma roasting on spits and Arabic coffee fresh off the fire. These smells mingled with minty hookah smoke dancing in the streets, just like the chaotic cars that knew no traffic lanes and tempted the fates of any pedestrians who dared cross the roads. The shouts and honks of traffic had their own rhythm against the sounds of Arabic music wafting in through the van windows, only to be drowned out by my uncle turning up the recitation of the Qur'an emanating from his car radio. All the stores flashed colorful, brightly lit signs in Arabic in bold text, or cursive font, or were transliterated in almost unreadable English letters. The pedestrian walkways could barely contain the throngs of people out and about on that Amman night. There were Jordanian women who looked like they'd stepped out of a European fashion catalog or window display, sporting dyed blond hair and wearing tight, faded jeans and colorful tube tops. They created a modern mosaic among more women who were covered head to toe in white or black veils and neutral-colored long robes, as well as trendy young hijabis in eye-catching headscarves and matching tunics and heels. The adults tripped over gleeful children in summer clothes as they played games of tag, or soccer, or with new toys right on the sidewalk. Young men with gelled hair, wearing button-up dress shirts and polos, chain-smoked their cigarettes on street corners and catcalled pretty girls, occasionally catching the glares of overprotective fathers with big beards walking past them with female members of their household. At one stop light, where we found ourselves gridlocked bumper to bumper with the rest of Jordanian traffic, the van right next to us was just as packed with men—one of whom held a *tabla*, or Arabic drum, on which he played an impossible beat that ignited the rest of his company in a loud song, rocking their vehicle back and forth with off-key lyrics and uncontainable laughter.

It wasn't until we pulled into my uncle's parking lot that my little brother Ameer realized the man driving us was our relative and not a taxi driver. When we climbed out of his van, we were once again hit by the ever-present smell of gasoline before being suddenly surrounded by a flurry of my cousins and aunts and uncles. They pulled us into eager embraces and planted sloppy kisses all over our faces. Each one of them introduced themselves to us in a frenzy of names and faces that would take me days to remember. Except for one girl who surfaced before me like a long-lost sister I had always known but never met.

"Do you know who I am?" she asked, her big beautiful brown eyes blinking long lashes at me, the same shade of reddish brown as the forelock of hair peeking from beneath a prayer scarf that she had thrown on in a hurry to meet us outside. "I'm Serein."

Of course I knew who Serein was. She had stolen my name. Or, rather, her parents had. She and I were the same age, living our separate lives on opposite parts of the world, only to hear about each other growing up through my father's stories from family visits to Jordan through the years. She was born months before me, so her parents were able to steal the beautiful name that my dad had originally picked for me. Serein. I always regretted that I could have been called a variant of Serena—the civilian name of my favorite childhood superhero, *Sailor Moon*. Almost poetically, Serein's face was a milky tone that, for the many coming months that we'd become inseparable, would inspire her suitors and admirers to compare her visage to the moon.

My older male cousins rushed to carry our luggage upstairs as more family led us to where dinner was waiting. As soon as I ascended the staircase, I was hit by the intense smell of Middle Eastern home cooking that was like both my mom's and grandma's kitchens on steroids. Serein's mom welcomed us into the largest room in the house, where the biggest silver platter I had ever seen was set on the ground and appeared to take up the circumference of the room. The platter was filled to the rim with rice, yogurt, goat, almonds, and parsley—a delectable Levantine concoction called *mansaf*. Dozens more relatives jumped to their feet to greet us, introduce themselves, and immediately seat us on the carpet at the edge of the platter so we could eat, insisting that we must be famished from our long trip. When I asked in English where the utensils were, and my dad said that we were to eat the *mansaf* with our hands, I was so overwhelmed by the culture shock that I politely excused myself and ran into Serein's nearby pink and white bedroom. That first night, she and I stayed up until dawn, when the morning call to prayer echoed in the empty streets, filling each other in on everything we had missed from each other's lives before we finally met.

Though we were technically the same age, through the help of Serein's schoolteacher mother she was able to skip a grade, so she was always one year smarter and one year wiser than me. She vehemently valued her education—eventually earning the highest degree in our extended family—and took great pride in the power it wielded, *especially* among her male counterparts. She never lived outside of the Middle East, yet somehow spoke perfect English, and she acted as both my translator and tutor, as well as my inspiration, to master my eventual bilingualism in school. She not only translated the language for me, but also the culture: Serein respected culture but not tradition. She was already well-versed in my lifestyle from all the English movies and music videos she watched on her family's American satellite. Our friendship kicked off with us exchanging the most popular music from our respective societies: I introduced her to Gwen Stefani's "Hollaback Girl," Mariah Carey's "We Belong Together," and Ciara's "1, 2, Step"; she introduced me to Nancy Ajram's entire *Ah W Noss* hit album, Tamer Hosny's "Kol Mara," and, at the time controversially risqué female singer Ruby and her hit single "Leih Bedary Keda." She taught me how to use public transportation and assertively ask the bus driver for my change back on a large bill.

One afternoon when she came home from school, she showed me the nearby Internet cafes in her neighborhood where teens would go to send secret messages to their lovers. Late one night at her house, while her parents slept in the next room, we snuck into her brothers' bedroom-turned-video game den where the boys were up playing *Dragon Ball Z* on my little brother Faris's coveted Play-Station 2. Serein had the exciting idea for all of us to pool together our money and quietly send one of her little brothers down to the late-night corner store to buy us soda and snacks to enjoy among ourselves—a rare indulgence in her busy household. When her older brothers bullied or disrespected me, she would be the one to mediate with timeless grace and self-assuredness.

It was on Serein's rooftop, overlooking the neighborhood mosque right next door, that I met Tamara in the cool blue twilight of the setting Middle Eastern sun. I remember it creating a purplish tint on her head as it gleamed off her dark brown hair, precariously revealed in plain sight with her headscarf undone and settled around her shoulders. Tamara's headscarf always inevitably found its way off her head. She was our oldest female cousin on my dad's side of the family, the daughter of his eldest brother, Ummo Yahya. Ummo Yahya was really strict and conservative, two attributes that met Tamara's young and indomitable Arab woman's spirit to ignite total rebellion. Serein spared me no hilarious or badass story of her adventures with Tamara growing up. Tamara always dramatically lined her hazel eyes with heavy, authentic kohl that stung when applied and was as black as the long, outwardly modest dark robes that she wore to conceal the tight outfits underneath. She never consistently went to school, busied by housework and early marriage instead, and had crooked teeth that knew not what biting her tongue meant. Her voice was deep and, to some, almost offensively loud in public spaces when it so-called immodestly attracted the attention of men in the street. Still in her twenties, she had already married and divorced a number of times—one divorce was already taboo enough for some people—because she had absolutely no problem walking away from Arab men, even husbands, who did not treat her with the respect she demanded. And she had no problem commanding the opposite sex, either. Many men were eager to impress and cater to her, and her uninhibited pride in her sexuality became a lightning rod of contention among conservative members of our extended family.

One night, during a dinner party we were hosting for our relatives, Tamara decided to disappear. Immediately upon discovering that Tamara was nowhere to be found, everyone concluded that she had a boyfriend pick her up in his car. Serein and I assumed she was out on a joyride. But, just like that, the entire conversation at the dinner party shifted the central focus to Tamara. Everyone was upset, everyone was talking about her, everyone was sharing their contempt for what they quickly assumed was inappropriate behavior. After being gone for what seemed like hours, Tamara casually strolled in through the front door without her usual headscarf, walked past the dining room full of family who watched her with their mouths agape, and took a seat on a floor cushion in the living room like nothing had happened. When we all rushed to ask where she had been, she expertly said, "What are you all talking about? I was hanging around the house the entire time." She grabbed her crumpled-up black scarf from a nearby cushion and held it up to us. "Look! My hijab was still here." Serein and I later learned that when Tamara came back from wherever she had gone, she took her headscarf off before reentering the house, and threw it into the room through an open window to plant her evidence. She knew the game all too well.

During my stay in Jordan, especially at the young age of thirteen, the culture shock compelled me to seek the easy security of wearing social expectations like a jacket. When Tamara drew the ire of our family, I often blamed her, questioning why she had to behave in a way that upset everyone around us. Did she really have to attract everyone's unwarranted and often destructive attention? Yet, at the same time, her presence became my escape. When I wanted to play soccer with the teen boys in the field behind my house, which, in our conservative neighborhood, might have been seen as inappropriate, she would come with me, befriending the entire neighborhood team. Everyone would fall in love with her from the moment they met her, magnetized by her intentional abandon of gendered propriety. She made crude jokes that automatically afforded her an "in" with the guys and she had a boisterous laugh that became a calling signal for the rest of the neighborhood kids to join us whenever we went to the soccer field. It eventually became so that the soccer field was at its most crowded and excitable when Tamara was around, and when she wasn't, all the boys stalled their desultory game, hoping she would show up. Being around Tamara allowed me to come alive and be myself again, to do what I wanted outside the constraints of the cultural expectations that made adjusting so difficult for me. I happily discovered that Tamara hadn't changed when I reunited with her again years later, on one of my college research trips to Jordan, when I wanted to sneak away from her father's household and meet a visiting guy friend from New Jersey at a restaurant on the other side of Amman. As soon as our fathers left her house for the day, we did our makeup and got dressed, called a taxi, and, just like the old days, went to meet up with the boy. Our fathers inevitably ended up returning home before us, and, upon discovering our absence, called Tamara's cell phone in total confusion about our whereabouts. As I grew older, the way that I became socially conditioned to see Tamara transformed into not just appreciation, but also deep admiration of her strength, resilience, and defiant assertion of the power of her womanhood.

Upon starting school in Jordan and meeting the other girls in my grade, I found they were curious about me, too. "You're from America? Aren't you supposed to be wearing a miniskirt?" was one of the first questions I was asked. They wanted to know how many Muslims were in my town, if I prayed or went to the mosque, and assumed I didn't fast during Ramadan. They wanted to know about boys and my experiences, an area in which I'm pretty sure I disappointed them. Actually, many of these girls were much more experienced than me in a lot of things. I found that many of them eagerly sought the type of lifestyle they imagined American girls lived, while I, a real American girl, was eager to experience an authentic culture I'd never had. At the same time, many Jordanians cared deeply about the "opinion" I would deliver of their country back to the United States upon my return. "Make us look good!" they would tell me, making me feel quite sad. "Let them know we're not like what they think we are!"

Jordan made me acutely aware of the privileges I had in the United States, and, even more so, the liberties I took for granted. I had a harrowing experience one day in school that I believe had a tremendous impact on the way I would use my voice upon my return to New Jersey. Our class leader, a super abrasive girl with long tight black curls, was standing by the bookshelves at the front of our classroom one morning, unraveling a large poster that was the portrait of a man. From afar, I could see that he was wearing a normal-looking jacket and had an unkempt beard and grown-out hair. To my thirteen-year-old self, it didn't look like a very flattering picture. From my seat in the back of the class, I exclaimed, in Arabic, "Ewww, who is that?"

In that moment, it seemed like side conversations, note reviewing, and doodling came to a screeching halt, and every single girl stopped what she was doing and turned back to look at me.

The class leader held up the poster and said in a horribly offended tone, "That is KING ABDULLAH!"

Damn. I guess he was going for the whole "of the people"–type of look in that one.

King Abdullah II bin Al Hashemi is the monarch of Jordan, who married a Palestinian commoner who became known to the world and her people as the beloved Queen Rania. King Abdullah succeeded his father, King Hussein, who was wildly popular among Jordanians. I used to think it was cool to see Queen Rania as an elegant, eloquent, and seemingly "modern"—for Western tastes—Muslim woman leader in the media, championing women's rights, until I started learning more about the many issues of inequity that still pervaded our country. Many years later, after the Arab Spring—the series of uprisings that flared up across the Middle East after the Tunisian and Egyptian revolutions in 2011—took off at the beginning of my freshman year of college, I would return to Jordan annually, eager to conduct independent research on the ground for Rutgers University. I wanted to explore the Jordanian youth and underground resistance movements and their demands of their government, and the more I learned, the more I resented the monarchy for the ways it suppressed them.

Immediately, all the girls in my class concluded that I would be kicked out of the school, and the class leader clamored to report me to the principal. What I said was perceived among these young girls to be an insurmountable offense, even though I had merely insulted authority in the most innocent, superficial way. It was through this interaction that I became awakened to just how privileged I was and how deeply I took my freedom of speech for granted living in the States. Upon my return to New Jersey, that was definitely a right that I planned to use fully, if only in response to the threat of me being deprived of it in Jordan.

Our stay in Jordan—which was supposed to last until I graduated high school—was fatefully cut short. My mother had caught E. coli. Unbeknownst to us, during the days that I was running around with Serein and Tamara, she was lying immobile with sickness on the floor cushions of our new home, her kidneys slowly failing her and she was dying. It wasn't until she was rushed to the hospital that we discovered something was terribly wrong, and my father felt it necessary for us to return to the States for my mother to be comforted by her relatives in New Jersey as she recovered. By then, the E. coli had eaten away at two discs in her spine, subjecting her to a decade of painful surgeries that almost cost her the ability to walk. For years after our return, my brothers and I would debate whether our trip to Jordan was really worth it.

On my last day of school in Jordan, I decided I wanted to say good-bye to all my new peers in front of the entire school during the morning lineup. That morning, my dad helped me write out a short speech in Arabic, and then transliterated it for me into English letters so I would be able to read it at a fast enough pace for my schoolmates to understand. (I was still slow in my Arabic reading, at that point.) I went to the front of the school, with all of the students from all the grades standing up in front of me, waiting to hear the one last thing that American girl had to say, and swallowed the lump in my throat. I told myself to just go. So I did.

"Thanks to you all, I'm leaving here having learned a lot of new things, and with a lot of new experiences," I told the overwhelming crowd before me. "And one thing that I'm taking back to America with me is something no one can take away. My hijab."

I was lucky in that my decision to wear the headscarf was a deeply personal and independent one. Up to that trip, I was so fractured by my Muslim identity and Western society that I was completely lost in this weird enigma of awkward girl puberty and unbearable racism that emerged as a total disconnect.

Being in Jordan was the first opportunity I had to learn about Islam in an accurate historical context among the people who practiced it. One of the classes we took in our public school was *deen*, or religion. When my tutor would come over after school, she would translate into English that day's lesson, filled with honorable battles and inexplicable miracles that reaffirmed my conviction in Islam. The culmination of my experience in Jordan, where I heard Muslim and Arab people's narratives and diverse stories in their own voices, reignited my pride in my heritage and religion and prompted my desire to finally reclaim my identity.

In one tutoring session after school, we were learning about the heroic Battle of Mu'tah. The battle was named after the city (coincidentally in Jordan) in which it took place almost 1,400 years ago, and had been immortalized as a tale of blind courage, cunning determination, and an almost unreasonable amount of faith. Prophet Muhammad, peace be upon him, sent his army of three thousand men, led by his dear companions, to confront the

Byzantine ruler who killed his peaceful messenger. Upon arrival, the companions discovered they were facing a Byzantine army of 100,000 soldiers. They hesitated, considered returning back to the prophet to report the impossible numbers, but then fearlessly chose to stay the course and move forward against all odds. A battle ensued that was decorated with moments of unlikely valor. The leaders of the Muslim army took turns carrying the banner of Islam and refused to drop it at any cost, while the Byzantine fighters aimed to cut it down. When the first leader carrying the banner was killed, the second leader instantly caught the banner before it fell to the ground, raising it back up into the air. As he fought, his right arm was cut off, but still this did not deter his resolve: he carried the banner with his left hand, until it, too, was cut off, at which point he used both of his upper arms to defiantly hold up the banner until he was killed. Then the next leader caught the banner and carried it to a similar fate.

One of the most famous fighters in Islamic history, Khalid ibn al-Walid—I learned that one of my Jordanian cousins was named after him—repositioned the Muslim army to attempt to trick the Byzantines. He ordered his forces to retreat behind a hill at night and return during the day, kicking up as much dust as possible to create the illusion that Muslim reinforcements had arrived. His idea worked, and the Byzantine army retreated, allowing the remaining Muslim soldiers to safely return home. Even though the battle wasn't considered a victory, it was far from a loss: in fact, it showed both the Muslims and the rest of the region the unimaginable force of faith.[1]

Listening to my tutor tell me the story, I was overwhelmed

---

1 Hadeer Shwket, "The Battle of Muta," MuslimGirl.com, August 28, 2010, http://muslimgirl .com/2445/battle-of-muta/.

with such pride in my history that I decided in that moment that I wanted to wear a headscarf, as a public marker that I belonged to this people. I wanted it to be so that before people even knew my name, the first thing that they would know about me is that I am a Muslim. I told myself that upon my return to the States, I would wear the headscarf with pride as my outward rebellion against the Islamophobia that had seized me and suffocated me for most of my life. With that decision, I inherited the entire history to which the hijab has been tied, and carried it on my head like an issue for public debate.

Throughout time, the headscarf has evolved to symbolize autonomy and control over Muslim women's bodies. An empowering rejection of the male gaze, colonialism, and anti-Muslim sentiment, it can just as easily be twisted into a disempowering tool of subjugation and repression through its forced imposition. In any given time period, the headscarf would be at the center of a tug-of-war between people and their governments, between colonizers and colonized people. During the French colonization of North Africa, the veil became an object of extreme sexualization, with white men writing literature fantasizing about ripping the scarf off sexy Arab women's heads—an act that became, in their minds, the most gratifying assertion of power. Edward Said taught us of the orientalized depiction of Middle Eastern women as seductresses hidden behind fictionalized harems—forbidden spaces kept for women only—that were a figment of the white man's imagination, an imagery that colonizers would stage for postcards to send back home to Europe. Today, some governments are just as eager to mandate its wear in public as others are to forbid it. In all cases, any decision to intervene in how a woman dresses, whether to take it off or put it on, is just the same assertion of public control over a woman's body. Iran's honor police enforce that all women wear a headscarf in public, while today's French laws forbid the veil in public schools. It's funny how, in our patriarchal world, even two entities at the opposite ends of the spectrum can be bonded by their treatment of women's bodies. Sexism has been employed in many ways throughout history to uphold racism.

Different cultures across decades and countries throughout the Muslim world treated the headscarf differently. Some of us have grandmothers who wore swimsuits to the beach in Egypt. Others of us, like me, might have been the first in our immediate family to put one on. It seems as though whenever there is a major attack against our identities, we see the pendulum of our generational relationship with the headscarf swing back toward reclaiming it. If this is the case, then it is evidence that the headscarf is not only intertwined with our respective cultures, but it has also become the strongest emblem of our distinct identities as Muslim women. And how could it not? It is hyper-visible and unmistakable.

In 2015, Chicago police attacked a Muslim woman wearing a headscarf and a face veil, suspicious of the food she was carrying in her purse to break her fast during Ramadan. They ripped the hijab off her head and strip-searched her, on video, which they then later released to the public. This wasn't just a random act of security. There is a feeling of entitlement to brown women's bodies, and her strip search—already an exertion of power over women—was compounded not just as an act of sexual humiliation, but also a racial one because of her ostensible religious identity.

Similarly, it is this exertion of power over our bodies that motivates TSA patdowns of headscarf wearers at airport security checkpoints. Think about it: We already have to walk through what is pretty much an X-Ray machine that allows you to see straight through our clothes. It is a monstrosity so invasive that, in 2011, there was a public outcry over a TSA whistle-blower's blog post in which he detailed how agents would ridicule the rolls of fat on passengers' bodies as the agents watched from their screening rooms.[2] Surely the headscarf is not made of some fabric that can defy such a machine, but nonetheless we are always, always, always stopped for an extra patdown, with TSA hands invariably laying claim to our bodies. The search isn't about security, but rather about hitting us where it hurts. As one TSA agent let slip to me during one of these encounters, "We have to check you if you're wearing that," and as another said on a separate occasion, "You've traveled with headgear before, right? So you know how this goes."

As a millennial woman in the post-9/11 era, I have truly felt that our generation has been the first to navigate this new plane of evolving Muslim identity and the unique issues we must face today. Growing up, I was a child with one foot in each door. I was born and raised within a diasporic culture that is not only detached from but warring with the region from which my parents hailed. In our home, my father did his best to envelop us within our native culture, maintaining the language and customs with which he himself was raised. I had to grow up with this hybrid sense of identity that's always somehow hyphenated. My responses of "I'm from New Jersey" are met with "But where are you *really* from?" Being bullied in school commonly made me resent parts of my heritage that other kids found weird, only to see them culturally appropriated a decade later as suddenly "cool." On top of it all, 9/11 happened when I was a child, and so I went through puberty at

2 Jason Edward Harrington, "Dear America, I Saw You Naked," Politico.com, January 2014, http://www.politico.com/magazine/story/2014/01/tsa-screener-confession-102912.

the height of modern-day Islamophobia. I was indoctrinated into a world of war from an early age: 9/11 happened when I was nine years old; we were well into the Afghanistan War when I turned ten; and by the time I was eleven, we had entered Iraq. I still remember Mrs. Rabii challenging our fifth-grade class with a trivia question in 2004: "What countries are we at war with right now?" Everyone knew we were at war with Iraq, but my classmates and I were stumped as to what the other country was—it turned out to be Afghanistan—and what exactly we were doing there. It is not an overstatement to say that 9/11, one of the worst attacks on our country in recent memory, for which followers of Islam were generically and collectively blamed, spawned a new age of double consciousness that impacted young American Muslims at a sensitive and vulnerable time in their developing lives.

Especially post-9/11, double consciousness manifested itself in the evolution of Muslim American engagement. Under microscopic scrutiny for terrorism and the collective expectation for us to constantly denounce, apologize, and take responsibility for the individual actions of extremists, we have severely internalized the public perception—empowered by media misrepresentation—of our communities as being made up of violent and crazy outsiders. As a result, we inadvertently prioritized shifting our image in the eyes of others rather than turning inward and cultivating our survival in this new trek we were forced to embark upon. I don't blame our community for this. I feel that the horrible scapegoating we've had to endure has forced us into a corner of defensiveness, dissipating our energy in this endless game of pushing back against the misconceptions that ultimately victimize us. Imperialism behaves in this way not only out of sheer contempt for peoples different than its own, but also in a deliberate effort to prevent these groups from building themselves up. It makes me sad to think about all the resources the Muslim American community has been forced to waste for the past decade on campaigns, events, and media efforts to prove that we, too, are American; that we, too, are *human*, begging and pleading the public to not believe the racist rhetoric being spewed about us. I can't imagine the types of institutions, programs, and civic society we could have cultivated for our community—the type of *backbone* we could have had the opportunity to grow—had we not been forced into this position.

In this way, our behavior—aimed at constantly combating stereotypes and unjustified hatred—centers, serves, and caters to the non-Muslims victimizing us, inevitably at our own expense. This has caused us to pretty much gag ourselves and tie our hands behind our backs so as to overcompensate for the judgments and try to convince the public that we are peaceful and harmless, much to our detriment. For example, when armed bikers decided to stage an anti-Muslim rally at a mosque in Phoenix, Arizona, in May 2015, Muslim community organizers who were discussing possible responses to the violence considered passing out bottles of water to the white men who wanted to annihilate our existence. While the community is entitled to determine the most fitting way for it to respond, it still stands that Muslims felt compelled to disempower themselves even further to showcase the peaceful nature of their religion in a situation that under any other circumstance would have required a strong head-on response for security. Many Muslims cite the behavior of our loving and compassionate Prophet Muhammad, peace be upon him, to justify such behavior, as it was his tradition to meet hostility with peace. But I think our attitude toward such docile responses would change drastically if we recognize them as still catering to those who would judge us.

My opinion is that the actual safety and sanctity of our community is under threat in moments like these, and that was something the Prophet never entertained; further, his acts of peace and turning the other cheek never came at the cost of human dignity.

One reason I believe that Muslim Girl has been so successful as a media outlet is because, for us, it was in this moment that we stopped seeking the attention of or affirmation from mainstream media about the issues that are important to us. For the first time, we didn't grovel at the feet of these media companies and beg them to cover our stories. Instead, we turned inward and made the conscious decision to develop our own alternative media channel. We released ourselves from the outward eye—by throwing ourselves straight into the center of it—and instead focused on engaging the conversations that were pertinent to our own interests and lived experiences. We created a moment for us to finally be introspective and cultivate our own identities, knowing that the world robbed us of the opportunity to do so when we were growing up. We wanted to fight stereotypes by being unapologetically ourselves and sharing what we had to say with the world. Our work has been built in the consciousness of a long line and tradition of Muslim women speaking truth to power, taking a central role in revolutionizing societies and propelling their respective generations forward toward emancipation. If we seem further along, it is by standing on the shoulders of superwomen.

Within this framework, *imagine* the experience of Muslim women whose headscarves publicly announce their religion. Forget the ISIS flag: When it comes to the outward eye, the hijab has become the flag of Islam. Because our racist society is quick to view minorities as monoliths, and because our sexist society is quick to reduce women to the attire they wear, Muslim women who wear headscarves have undoubtedly become the involuntary representatives of an entire religion. Following the irrational logic according to which Muslims are judged (i.e., if one Muslim commits terrorism, then all Muslims are terrorists), every action that a visibly identifiable Muslim woman takes in public is immediately attributed to our religion as a whole. In this way, we exist in the public sphere in a perpetual state of constant awareness and consciousness of the outward eye. Our actions are constantly manipulated, negotiated, and limited to serve that purpose—another manifestation of the oppression we suffer from Western society.

We are on the front lines of Islamophobia. Physical assault, hate crimes, and harassment against us are not only attacks upon us as individuals, but attacks on Islam itself. Like lightning rods, we attract and bear the brunt of the hateful attitudes, rhetoric, and media frenzies prompted by Islamophobia.

Chapter 3

On my first day back to junior high school in New Jersey in 2006, I had a panic attack.

I was walking to school with my dad that morning, wearing the headscarf that I had brought back with me from Jordan. It would be the first time I saw all my classmates again since leaving nine months earlier, and it would be the first time any of them saw me with a scarf on my head. For many of them, it would be their first time learning I was a Muslim. I was excited for this day to come, until it finally did, and then I was suddenly fighting butterflies in my stomach. A feeling of anxiety washed over me the closer we got to school, and then, as we were climbing up the grassy green lawn toward the baseball field, I froze dead in my tracks and broke into tears.

"What's wrong?" Baba asked, deeply concerned. "Amani, if you don't want to wear it to school, you don't have to. If it's going to be this hard for you, you can take it off."

I genuinely gave the option some thought. "I don't know what to do," I said. "I'm scared I'm going to lose my friends. What if everyone hates me? How will people treat me? If I walk in wearing a headscarf now, I feel like I'll never be able to take it off, and if I take it off now, I feel like it's going to be so much harder for me to put it back on."

I was already late to school. I needed to be decisive. I needed to be intentional.

"Whatever you want to do, I support you," my dad said to me. "Just know that if you are able to commit to this, then there's nothing else in your life that you wouldn't be strong enough to commit to."

I took a deep breath, wiped my face, looked back at the school, and readied myself for the moment that would change my life forever. "All right, let's go."

It was the image of Auntie Ebtisam, standing up from the raft at the bottom of the slide at Splash Zone, drenched clothes sticking to her skin, laughing from behind her black sunglasses and wet, lopsided hijab, that I remembered.

I was one of only a small handful of girls in my large high school who wore headscarves. During lunch I would be grateful just to find someone to sit with, regardless of the company. On my first day back to school in New Jersey after returning from Jordan, I spent my lunch hiding in a bathroom stall rather than facing the anxiety of finding a table to sit at, or, worse yet, sitting alone. The cafeteria pretty much defined which social circle you belonged to, and I guess it was an outward manifestation of my internal detachment and new cultural disorientation that I never had a defined table of my own. Walking into the cafeteria inevitably made me feel like all eyes were on me, and, in my severe reverse culture shock from returning to the States, that was a newfound attention that I was eager to shake off. I couldn't stand the prickly feeling of passing by a table with a lunch tray in my hands, clearly looking for a place to sit, only to be met with the unwelcoming glares of peers silently signaling that, no, a seat at their table was not available. Nor could I bring myself to ask, "Can I sit here?" and subject

myself to the unbearable scrutiny of whether I was socially acceptable enough. On top of my awkwardness, I felt like my headscarf
created a new barrier between me and the other students with
whom I wished to connect. This all came to a head when I was
walking home from school one day that year and a gang of girls
circled around me in the parking lot and tried to get me to take
my headscarf off. It was not long before I came to the conclu-
sion that if I wanted to survive, I had to force my personality out
to protect myself and overcome this barrier—that, if I wanted to
break out of it, I had better chances by being the one to extend my
hand and start the conversation. By eleventh and twelfth grade,
I relied on my wit to feel like I had some worth among my much
cooler peers, who could afford to wear a different Ed Hardy something every day and matching uniforms of Uggs and Abercrombie.
I came across as standoffish or condescending, but at least it was
something better than feeling worthless.

I guess my first very tangible experience of life post-hijab
came one humid afternoon in an inauspicious parking lot across
the street from my junior high. My mom had just picked me up
and we were on our way home. I was sitting in the passenger seat
in my super-awkward hijab—I still hadn't figured out what styles
were flattering for my chubby cheeks (if only I had appreciated
them more instead of totally resenting the way they made my face
look like a tomato in just about any scarf I tried at the time!)—
and she was driving with the windows down, as was her style my
entire life. I still remember looking up at her when I was much
younger and much shorter, seeing her bangs flutter in the breeze
as she smiled from behind her thick sunglasses and sang along to
a throwback '80s song.

My mom doesn't wear a headscarf, and I almost forgot how

shocking this is to some people. Even recently, I Instagrammed a photo of us from the Cannes Lions Festival in France and people flooded the comments asking how this could be and if we would make a video about our respective decisions. One commenter wrote, "I don't think I've ever seen a daughter that was traditional and her mother wasn't." It's a welcome observation: Personally, I just love how it seizes people's preconceived notions about the hijab and causes them to question the supposed compulsoriness of it all. The first time someone confronted me about it, it was the secretary in my high school principal's office, a friendly non-Muslim white woman who felt comfortable approaching me about these sensitive topics, and she pulled me aside one day to ask me why my mom didn't wear a scarf on her head.

"Because she doesn't want to," I flatly replied, prompting a subtle smile on her face. God bless her soul. I still remember the time she asked me why I was "Americanizing" my impossibly long last name by shortening it to the KATATBA printed across the back of my track hoodie. I was slightly offended that my decision would be presumed to have anything to do with being more "American," when honestly my last name exceeded the apparel character limit, as was typical. But what she said would always stick with me: "You should be emphasizing every single letter of your last name with pride, in all its cultured glory." Baby steps. I soon changed my profile name on Facebook from Amani Katatba to the abbreviated Amani Alkhat, much to the dismay of my peers, and then eventually to Amani Al-Khatahtbeh. In all its glory.

But back in that parking lot across the street from my junior high on that warm day, there were few things of which I was sure. We had just gotten pulled over by a cop car, the lights still in my mom's rearview mirror, and some white officer was now outside my mom's driver's-side door asking for her license and registration. She was navigating the conversation as smoothly as she normally does, asking what the trouble was and making small talk about the weather. But then the officer decided to bend down and peer in through the window, to look past my mom and right at me on the other side, sitting pensively in the passenger seat, with my unruly unibrow, my scarf haphazardly wrapped around my head. And then he said it.

"Do y'all speak English?" he interrupted my mom—clearly mid-conversation in her perfect I've-been-here-since-I-was-nine-years-old Jersey accent.

I can't tell you how I responded, because I really don't remember. My memories of that afternoon are doused with anger about how this dude had the audacity to ask me if I spoke English when I probably spoke it better than him. I started reading when I was a toddler; by the time I was in first grade, I was getting called out of English class to join a special instructor because I read faster than all my peers; by fourth grade, I was part of the Talented and Gifted program for advanced students, and once I reached middle school, I was placed in advanced English classes, where I'd remained ever since. That year, upon my return from Jordan, I had to argue to my junior high guidance counselor about why I needed to be placed in a higher level of English because I had already read all the books in my class's curriculum that year. And now I was facing this prejudiced asshole who took one look at the scarf on my head and assumed that I didn't belong, and thus that I could not speak English.

I wish I could say that experience was out of the norm, but it truly was the first of many similar encounters since I made the commitment to wear a headscarf. Another time in college, I was shopping in the makeup aisle of a drugstore—probably for more contour powder or something, naturally—and a white woman shopping beside me was struggling to read the back of a bottle. "Excuse me—" she started, in a thick European accent, until she looked up from the product to see me in all my hijabi glory, and was startled. "Oh! Sorry, do you speak English?"

I'm not sure how many times is the norm for the "average American" to be asked if she speaks English while living in, you know, presumably English-speaking America, but I'm guessing that number substantially increases if you fall within one of the following categories: 1) You have a shade of skin that is not considered white. 2) You wear garments that connect you with a certain culture or religion, and more so if that culture or religion is flagrantly misrepresented by the media. 3) You are actually visibly an out-of-place tourist or something. Taking into account the large number of minority communities we have in our country, I am going to take the guess that many of us, from many different backgrounds, have been subjected to the same scrutiny.

This type of experience demonstrates some very deeply entrenched preconceptions that American society harbors toward its minority communities. The assumption that one cannot speak English because of one's culture or religion stems from historical stereotypes of immigrants—specifically, people of color—as being uneducated, illiterate, unintelligent, and unassimilated. And seeing as how America should be the "salad bowl" of the modern world, it doesn't make sense that being "unassimilated" should be seen as unordinary or viewed so negatively in today's society.

I'm not sure if every young person experiences a moment when they are confronted, point-blank, by their own naiveté, when it shakes them awake and dissolves that fantastical dream of how big the world is and their sheer power to possess it. If *To Kill a Mockingbird* is any signifier, there is likely a moment in which we lose our innocence, and that doesn't necessarily have to mean engaging in an act that is constructed to be adulterated. I still painfully remember what that moment was for me. It wasn't in the deaths of Muhammad and Jamal al-Durrah, which I watched on my parents' Arabic satellite television in the warm living room of our New Jersey home when I was only eight years old. That may have represented my first tangible exposure to senseless violence—even though, at the time, I still didn't fully understand why they died or who had killed them. I was only cued to sadness in school the next day when my teacher, knowing my mother was Palestinian, came up to me to ask if I had watched the horrible scene and how tragic it was. Well, it was hard to avoid. Muhammad and Jamal—in the since repeated image of Jamal desperately covering his twelve-year-old son Muhammad with his arm under ceaseless crossfire before both were shot dead—became a symbol of innocent life cut short, of the pure humane instinct to protect rendered obsolete.

No, that moment of lost innocence would come much later, during the start of the year in which I would finally create Muslim Girl.

I don't remember where I was when I first got the news about Operation Cast Lead being under way, but I will likely never forget how I spent the duration of it. It was an Israeli ground invasion in Gaza at the end of 2008 that was a response to Hamas rocket fire against the occupation. The civilian population of Gaza, one of the most densely populated territories in the world, was unarmed due to a long-standing blockade that stopped any raw materials from entering the country. Meanwhile, the Israeli army utilized weapons that were outlawed according to international law. This was an unbearable attack for me to witness. It happened exactly during winter break of my junior year in high school. It was also during the lame-duck period leading up to President Barack Obama's inauguration following a successful presidential campaign, the first for which I volunteered. I dedicated my whole heart to the effort, and would walk around our track during gym class listening to its anthem "Yes We Can" by will.i.am. I do remember President Obama being my hero yet remaining conveniently silent about the whole ordeal while he vacationed in Hawaii with his family before dealing with the human tragedy he was about to inherit. Operation Cast Lead was the first military ground invasion in Occupied Palestine that I was old enough to witness, understand, and feel.

I spent my winter vacation with the television tuned to the news, nonstop, and my eyes were glued to the constant coverage of the operation. As I watched the casualty count continue to rise beyond my control, I remember that that was the first time I felt utterly powerless. My entire young life up until that point, I had this insurmountable idea that I was going to change the world. Having grown up through the Iraq and Afghanistan wars, having watched Muhammad and Jamal on my television set, I told myself that I wanted to stop a war from happening—to prevent the senseless deaths of innocent people. And now I was watching them happen right before my eyes, and the wind was knocked right out of me.

December 30, 2008 @ 8:14 a.m.

My eyes are welling up with tears just typing this out, and I can't even cry about it because then I feel guilty for crying about it and wallowing in my own self-pity while hundreds of people are dying. I've never felt so helpless in my entire life. I've always preached that things are in our control, not the government's, and yet here I am, finding myself face-to-face with a huge fucking wall that has "THIS IS THE WAY THINGS ARE" written on it in big red letters.

The counts were depressing. Total Israelis killed: 13. Total Palestinians killed: 1,417. The disproportionate response was denounced by human rights organizations globally. Yet, the way the media slanted its coverage of the conflict was wildly unfair. When there were Israeli casualties, they were "soldiers murdered." When there were Palestinian casualties, they were "terrorists killed." There was no discussion of the context of the conflict—no remorse, or even distinction, regarding the civilians killed, many of whom were women and children. The public wasn't moved. Any public discussion rested on "But they started it," and that was that. It was then that I witnessed how media misrepresentation can directly empower violence abroad.

The way Palestinian women especially were misrepresented by the media was heartbreaking for me, and displayed how directly women were viewed as an extension of their nation and, thereby, a justification of actions against it. Years later, while working my first post-grad job as the media relations specialist of the American-Arab Anti-Discrimination Committee in Washington, DC, I would be confronted by this again during another Israeli military operation in Gaza, this time called Operation Protective Edge, in 2014. It was Israel's response to three young Israeli men being kidnapped in a settlement. During a time of heightened sensitivity, the *Wall Street Journal* published an article titled, "Where

Are the Palestinian Mothers?" which argued, based off the writer's interactions with three women, that all Palestinian mothers raised their sons to be suicide bombers and were eager to have their children's lives claimed by martyrdom—and thus that the Palestinian people required "moral rehabilitation." On top of being blatantly racist, the rhetoric sought to justify the disproportionate violence inflicted on the bodies of Palestinian women and children. By mischaracterizing, and then generalizing, Palestinian women in this way, it first dehumanized them, and then turned them into symbols of the people as a whole in a political attempt to normalize the idea of collective punishment by a state against a people.

Similarly, Afghan women received the same type of processed treatment to justify the Afghanistan War that turned the lives of countless little Muslim girls around the world upside down. First Lady Laura Bush delivered an iconic speech in 2001 in which she virtually rewrote and maneuvered Afghan women's narratives on their behalf.[1] In an attempt to rally public support for military intervention, Laura Bush called on the American people to liberate Afghan women from the oppression of what she deemed to be a backward civilization:

> Civilized people throughout the world are speaking out in horror—not only because our hearts break for the women and children in Afghanistan, but also because in Afghanistan we see the world the terrorists would like to impose on the rest of us. . . . We will be especially thankful for all the blessings of American life. I hope Americans will join our

1 Laura Bush, "Radio Address by Mrs. Bush," The American Presidency Project, November 17, 2001, http://www.presidency.ucsb.edu/ws/?pid=24992.

family in working to insure that dignity and opportunity will be secured for all the women and children of Afghanistan.

While individual liberties were overwhelmingly suppressed by the Taliban, she used the Afghan women's narrative to impose a violent solution that was not of their own choice or opinion, and which, in retrospect, placed even more devastation upon them by subjecting them to war and disproportionately harming them and their children. The theft of brown women's narratives is not only an injustice placed on them, but also one extended to their male counterparts; by insisting they need to be liberated from their "barbaric" civilization, Laura summoned the colonial assertion that brown women need saving from brown men, when, in actuality, brown women have suffered at the hands of white men more than at those of any other oppressor in history. It is this mentality that makes it easier to understand how the United States government could commit such inhumane acts like those perpetrated in the Abu Ghraib prison cells or at the Guantánamo Bay detainment center.

I was one of a seemingly small minority of Muslim students in our huge high school of three thousand students in conservative Republican East Brunswick, New Jersey. During media frenzies surrounding Islam or Muslims around the world, I was usually one of the only voices against what I believed to be human rights atrocities, much to my own ostracization, even from teachers. In eleventh grade, I had a history teacher named Mr. A. He was one of the youngest teachers in the department, with a hilariously sarcastic sense of humor that kept my attention in what became my favorite class of the day because of the topic area. That year, as part of the curriculum on U.S. history, we were learning about the Iraq War of 2003. I'm not sure if he was the one who brought up the subject or if I did by the sheer absence of it from the lesson, but during one class period, we talked about Abu Ghraib.

The Abu Ghraib scandal was one of major significance to me growing up. It came to light when I was still a teenager, and it does something to you to see people who look like your family get tossed in naked piles of limbs and genitals like animals. It absolutely unnerved me as an Arab Muslim girl, reminding me that still today my own society saw me as nothing more than a brown body that only belonged in another world. The blatant usurping of power stunned me, affirming that it was true: They could do whatever they wanted to us. We were the barbarians from a backward, inhuman civilization. We were the savages with no respect for life or human dignity, apparently.

"The U.S. government tortured these Iraqis in a prison cell and used tactics especially offensive to their Muslim faith," I shared with Mr. A and my class from my seat. In my high school I always felt obligated to be the voice to speak up against injustices that were being swept under the rug through our school system. I would be vindicated three years later, when I'd be invited to guest teach an honors history class about Islamophobia under the supervision of the district's history supervisor. I'd point to the dusty history textbooks lining the wall of a class full of bright, wide-eyed young people and tell them, "Everything you're learning here is bullshit."

Mr. A responded with: "They got what they deserved. They're all terrorists."

I can imagine feeling that punch in the gut I still get whenever I hear something blatantly dehumanizing and just *wrong*, which never hurts any less no matter how many times you hear it. How can it hurt any less each time you are told you are inferior?

"No, they're not. They're Iraqi civilians," I pushed back.

"*Yeah,* Amani, because the American military really just rounded up random Iraqis off the streets and threw them in these jails, right?" he said in a sarcastic tone that prompted the entire class to erupt with laughter. In that moment I might have almost second-guessed myself. It *was* a wild assertion, but not because I was wrong; it was because our actions overseas really were that horrific, and our complacency at home really was that outrageous. In situations such as those—which arose pretty often in my conservative suburban high school, as you might imagine—I felt obligated, as the often sole dissenting voice, to deliver these marginalized narratives to my classrooms. My Islamic faith taught me that if you can't change something with your hands, change it with your tongue, and if you can't change it with your tongue, then desire to change it in your heart. Injustices were taking place under our noses, often financed by our tax dollars, and the absolute *least* we could do was muster up the courage to speak up about them when the opportunity arose.

That day after school, I went to the computer lab to use EBSCOhost to search the topic of Abu Ghraib's prisons for some semblance of the truth that I'd insisted upon in our classroom earlier that day. I still remember the somber feeling that washed over me as I scrolled through the pages and pages of torture photos that popped up on my screen. The reminder of the injustice only emboldened my search. Then I found it: the Holy Grail. A research report *said,* outright, that the American military rounded up random Iraqi civilians off the streets into the backs of their trucks and dumped them into this monstrous prison, without bringing a single charge against most of them.[2] In one article for the *New*

2 Seymour M. Hersh, "Torture at Abu Ghraib," *New Yorker*, May 10, 2004, http://www .newyorker.com/magazine/2004/05/10/torture-at-abu-ghraib.

Yorker, Pulitzer Prize–winning journalist Seymour M. Hersh described most of the prisoners, including women and teenagers, as being "civilians, many of whom had been picked up in random military sweeps and at highway checkpoints." I printed out the thick packet of research and carefully highlighted the parts that directly disputed the points that Mr. A had gotten the whole class laughing about.

The next day I was eager to show Mr. A what I'd found. I handed him the packet, opening to the page about the rounding up off the streets, the trucks with impunity, the no charges. He read it, squinted his eyes, and said, "It depends on how you read the sentence," as if I was the one who couldn't understand basic English.

Toward the latter part of high school, the paralyzing way I viewed myself came to be seen as being standoffish by the rest of my peers. I could no longer connect with people. I found it painfully awkward to be in social settings, and I experienced such an intense feeling of disconnect that I couldn't even identify basic social cues, like to laugh when someone in class said something funny. It's difficult to describe—it was like the conversations happening around me didn't apply to me. I wasn't good enough. I was suffering from a mix of an inferiority complex and a racialized imposter syndrome; I feared I would be outed as undeserving of being here among the rest. I was made to believe I actually wasn't as smart, or as hardworking, or as worthy. Of course, as the law of attraction would have it, my peers treated me the same way I was expecting to be treated, which only affirmed how I felt. I was an outcast and I didn't belong.

To add insult to injury, the male high school teacher of my

competitive political program and Model United Nations class took me aside one day to have a talk with me, in which he told me, point-blank, that I was "very large. Just *big*—" and thus intimidating to everyone else in my class. "You have to smile more and be more bouncy," he advised me, to counteract my intimidating behemoth of a body and earn my classmates' civility. He was the same teacher who, for my senior Model United Nations conference—the capstone trip for all participating seniors before graduation—paired me with a *sophomore* who was the only other girl in our program who wore a headscarf. Pairing a senior with a sophomore—even for a regular Model UN conference, let alone the final competition for a senior—was unusual, and something that had never been done before. My level was reduced to that of a first-year in the program, and, again, it was my headscarf that became the most important criterion and marker of my level relative to those around me.

That all came to a head at the end of senior year—the year I founded Muslim Girl—right before graduation in 2010. I actually threw my hat in the ring to go to prom. For some reason, I assumed all through high school that I wasn't going. Things like that weren't for *me*. But, I guess, like the question Mrs. Rabii posed to me all those years prior, I thought, *Why not?* I wanted to go to prom. And so I started shopping for a plus-size dress off a clearance rack at the mall and figuring out how I would style my already difficult headscarf for a formal affair. I found a dress that not only fit me, but was also kind of flattering and made me feel confident—in my favorite shade of purple, no less. It had a silver rhinestone embellishment on it, so I bought sparkly silver high-heeled shoes, which were probably the fanciest shoes I had ever owned at that point. Then, finally, I hunted for days and eventually found a black scarf with glittery silver trim that went with my black bolero jacket—gotta cover those arms, you know—and pulled the entire outfit together.

One of my classmates needed one more person to split the cost of a limousine, and that's how I earned my spot in actual pre-prom plans, with photos and everything. We were to meet up at my classmate's extravagant home in an affluent community, where the other girls in our group would be waiting with their dates, and my classmate's mom would serve red wine for the grown-ups to enjoy and commemorate the special occasion, before it was picture-taking time.

To regard something with such importance was, to me, a symbol of esteem, and before I decided to attend prom I truly didn't think I was "in the running" or worthy enough to have the experience. It was a radical act for me to consider that I should go. That thought of not being "in the running" was one that permeated other facets of my self-image, such as where my shapely, big, brown body was concerned. It wasn't like white girls' bodies. It wasn't normal. It didn't have a slim waist that tapered into seemly hips and a refined butt. I was a gigantic blob who loomed over people, in doorways—who was, in the way I saw myself, always in the way. Mine wasn't a woman's body—it didn't look like the bodies I saw on TV.

The day of prom, my mother employed her hairstylist friend to come over to our house and do my makeup in preparation for the big night. I spent hours getting ready—from the pampering, to the press-on nails and pedicure, to plucking away at the unibrow before sliding on the shiny new dress, to, finally, fashioning my fancy headscarf with a rhinestone headband to top it off. My dad even closed his electronics store early—it took something SERIOUS for *that* to happen!—to give me my share of the limousine tab and drive me to my friend's home.

We drove up to her gorgeous white house, and my dad pulled over to drop me off. "You look great!" he reassured me, as I said thank you, bid him farewell, and jumped down from his van. As I closed the door behind me and started walking toward her steps, a weird feeling seized me by the throat. I freaked out. I stopped dead in my tracks, turned around, ran back, and opened the passenger-side door of Baba's van, and, in tears, told him that I didn't want to go.

He seemed taken aback by my sudden shift in emotion, and then almost angry. "Baba, you are good enough," he said. "You are worthy enough to be with them. Don't think you're not." I didn't realize at the time that that was what I needed to hear, or that feeling less than enough was where my negative reaction came from. It took many more years of self-awareness for me to learn what he meant when he said that to me, or the roots of what I felt that day. But I did go to prom, in all my single and grape-purple glory, and I insisted on being part of the prom photos with the couples in their corny prom poses, as I awkwardly stood on the edge of the lineup, hand on my hip, against a shiny white limousine.

My dad always had this eerie way of knowing how I was feeling even when I didn't. In my reaction to prom, it was like he had it all figured out, and it took me years to realize that he probably knew because he saw in me something that he too harbored within himself.

Unlike how Baba didn't think twice about identifying my lack of self-worth, I didn't question why, that evening, he didn't park the car, hop out, and come join the rest of the parents in my classmate's kitchen, where they were happily socializing, talking proudly about the great night their kids were about to have. He didn't belong among them. Even though he still remained close to his childhood friend Mamoun in Jordan, it was difficult for him to socialize himself in America. Ever since I could remember, my father had worked in his electronics store every single day, from morning until night, to make ends meet for our family. Any day that he was forced to close the store meant we might not be able to pay a bill or make a grocery run. As an immigrant from a low-income background, my father didn't have the privilege of a social life. Actually, he rarely connected with people deeply enough to make friends. Most of the people with whom he socialized were his employees, and even they routinely betrayed his trust by shoplifting from his store when he wasn't looking. His best friend in America was an old Jewish man named Eddie Cohen who owned a kosher hot dog stand in the same flea market where my dad had a video game store, and they didn't get along at first. But over the years, they became such close and seemingly unlikely companions that when Eddie died from a sudden heart attack, I realized I hadn't seen my dad mourn that deeply for anyone since his father passed away.

It wasn't until I got older that I started noticing that my dad exhibited the same type of behavior, that same type of internalized disqualification from the running. His own self-image could be considered a reflection of the immigrant experience, the most basic premise of which was the underlying assumption that if you left your home country for here, then your home country is inferior. Meanwhile, we have selective memory and conveniently forget that Western countries are often to blame for the issues prompting immigration in the first place.

As Muslim Girl's work started gaining more and more attention, I was invited to a beautiful event among prestigious company,
and of course I invited my parents to join me and enjoy the night.
(As the daughter of immigrants, I know my people feel me when I
talk about how much it means to us to bring our parents along to
revel in our success. My mother said, "I feel like God is rewarding
me for the all the hardship I've been through." That was enough.)
At the end of what I thought was a really pleasant evening, we
were walking to the car and my dad said, in a self-deprecating
tone, "I guess we were able to squeeze ourselves among company
like that tonight!" My happiness that evening instantly deflated
in that moment. His comment was steeped in what I thought was
self-loathing, a sheer feeling of worthlessness and undeservingness
by comparison.

But the way I received his remark—with not just sadness this
time, but almost with anger, with offense—hinted to me that I saw
it as an insult to myself and my work. By extension, that revile-
ment meant that somewhere deep down, I was starting to believe
in my own worth, that I did deserve to take up this space, that
my people's accomplishments were worthy. And our self-esteem,
the way we regarded ourselves as we navigated these spaces, was
worth more than anything.

Chapter 4

Reem, Diana, and I were eagerly counting down the minutes until it was *iftar* time—or time to break our fast after what we mutually agreed was a long Ramadan day. In the brief moments leading up to our first sip of water, Diana remarked, "This minute is longer than a minute on the stair climber," and I couldn't help but burst out laughing. We observed that this Ramadan was the longest fasting days that we had probably ever experienced. Reem and I graduated from high school together, and also attended Rutgers University together, where she became the vice president of Muslim Girl's first collegiate chapter, founded on our campus. We had planned events together, and I always admired how much esteem Reem gave her leadership position. Not only did she pick up *all* the slack whenever something needed to get done, but her killer outfits on our big nights were second to none. I loved watching her shine.

We were sitting in a booth in an Olive Garden in New Jersey, where we finally settled after dodging long lines at the Cheesecake Factory and a nearby Thai spot, and rushed to catch *iftar* (while we were waiting, we noticed droves of veiled Muslim women and their families file in, including two of our former classmates from college, who had been smart enough to make reservations ahead of time). Now we were squirming in Olive Garden's leather seats, taking in whiffs of the delicious basket full of freshly baked breadsticks, until—finally—it was time.

That's how I ended up with a mouthful of breadsticks when a

waiter from our section interrupted me: "Hey, excuse me, are you the founder of MuslimGirl.com?" Mid-chew, I responded, "Yes, I am," kind of shocked that someone would recognize me from the website here in my hometown, even at dinner. It had been happening more and more recently, but I never took it into any account. My little brother Ameer told me about a recent encounter at the bank, when the teller asked, "Are you Amani's brother? I recognize your last name." When he affirmed and asked if she knew me, she said, "Oh, no, I just really love what she's doing." It started to hit me when I got invited to the Halal Guys' grand opening, where the owners escorted me away from the line swirling around the block, introduced themselves, and fixed me and Ameer up with some free dinner. A couple of weeks earlier, I'd heard that one of my former high school teachers, who once said my writing was unimpressive, wanted to catch up with me. It was all pretty cool, especially since I'd started the website in high school, right here.

"I was at Clinton Global Initiative University, I heard you speak," the waiter said. "I thought you were amazing! The way you responded to Bill Clinton was just so cool. You spoke with so much power," he went on. We had a conversation in which he told me he was part of a group that had been selected to attend, and that was how he ended up there, and how he didn't think it was me because what would I be doing in New Jersey?

"My family lives up the street," I told him. Small world.

We wrapped up our conversation and he politely allowed us to return to our dinner. Reem asked, "Does that happen often?" I told her it was starting to. I was increasingly astonished and elated that the conversations we were starting on MuslimGirl.com were reaching audiences far and wide—in this case, a millennial white

Jewish man with blond hair and blue eyes, in the middle of suburban New Jersey.

I was sitting on the carpet of my bedroom floor in June 2008 when I decisively registered a new LiveJournal community called MuslimGirls. I was picking out a graphic of the Muslim opening line of the Qur'an, *Bismillah ir Rahman ir Raheem*, or, "In the name of God, the Most Gracious, the Most Merciful," to top our very first introductory post. Between an interesting geometric calligraphic design and an unconventional pink Arabic script that almost looked like graffiti, I went the unconventional route. It was important to me that every detail about MuslimGirls was unconventional: that it was unique and accessible to young girls and showed that Islam was cool and interesting. It had to be anything other than usual.

I would stay up all night that summer, accompanied by one of my best friends from the mosque, Maha Zayed. We would exchange ideas on MSN messenger of what our first community members would enjoy, bonding over deliriously sleep-deprived jokes until 4 a.m. "Maha, are you sure I shouldn't make the subject text PINK?" was the kind of question I would subject her to, alongside more characteristic ones like, "Not allowing guys is the best decision, right?" We were eager to create and nurture a space for ourselves, and we weren't quite sure how many people it would attract after we launched. We endeavored to make the space available, and looked forward to building bonds with new members, whether they numbered 10 or 100. Maha and six other women would later make up the first seven bloggers to launch the Muslim Girl blog after almost exactly one year.

The number one question reporters always ask me is, "How did you start Muslim Girl?" As one journalist from *Playboy* thoughtfully mentioned during a phone interview from LA, "You must get so sick of answering the same question, 'as a Muslim woman,' over and over again."

We started Muslim Girl much like millennials start anything these days: on the internet. I bought a seven- or nine-dollar domain name registration for a new website, my friend Erica from LiveJournal added it onto her hosting plan for free, I formed a virtual Muslim girl squad, and—voilà!—we started.

LiveJournal was a very active blogging platform in the early 2000s. If you're into internet legacy, or even just watched *The Social Network*, you might recognize LiveJournal as the site where Mark Zuckerberg (under his very fitting username "zuckonit") live-blogged his hacking of Harvard University's public student directory when he developed Facesmash, the early ancestor of what we now know as Facebook.

Before I knew who Mark Zuckerberg was and before I was cool enough (or old enough) to have my own Facebook profile, I was a user alongside him, around the same time I started teaching myself code and how to build websites. I was preoccupied with creating the grungiest backgrounds for my blog and coding my own layouts with HTML and CSS, often seeking inspiration from the other, more experienced graphic designers on there. I remember when I taught myself how to make animated GIFs from my dad's internet café on the boardwalk on the Jersey Shore, and spent weeks from then on obsessively trying to outdo my evolving skills to create cool user icons for my LiveJournal profile.

I might have been eleven years old on there, passing myself off as old enough to befriend and be added to other users' 18+ blogs. That was where I learned the concept of a pregnancy scare, an experience documented by a tall strawberry blonde girl I followed, who nervously asked her LiveJournal friends if she could get pregnant from having sex in the shower with her boyfriend. Always the sheltered and naïve one and far removed from developing a social life of my own, I deeply learned about relationships on LiveJournal, and intimately witnessed how insecurity was present within many of us.

LiveJournal is where I was first exposed to feminist, self-realized interpretations of Islam. At the time, bullying and anti-Muslim bigotry had stunted me so severely in terms of building connections that I eagerly sought those spaces online. I turned to the internet to discuss Muslim issues and search for a lived experience similar to my own. Mind you, I was a total loner. My days in high school were spent just short of being a solid outcast. I floated between different social circles without ever having one of my own. After school, I rarely—if *ever*—had any plans, except for that one year I decided to do winter track and got made fun of by the other prettier, thinner, faster girls in the locker room because I wheezed to keep up with them when I ran. Instead, I would recede to my LiveJournal when I got home, where I would chronicle the details of my life every single day. Most of the friends I had that I would talk to on a daily basis only existed online.

LiveJournal had a feature called "Communities," which were sort of like message boards you could become a member of to discuss specific topics with other like-minded users. There were few active Islamic communities on there, and I remember noticing that all the ones I could find were run by and comprised of Muslims much older than me, and usually had mixed memberships of both men and women. Very few discussions centered around women specifically, unless they were shallow conversations in which women were being mansplained to about how to practice

Islam correctly in their gendered circumstances. It wasn't different from many other spaces online for Muslims at the time: They were predominantly focused on jurisprudence—*halal* this, *haram* that—regarding topics I simply could not relate to, especially as a teenager. The problems I was facing as a Muslim girl growing up in America went far beyond a superficial discussion of how I should dress in public and the proper way to wrap my headscarf.

But then, one LiveJournal post changed everything. I remember stumbling upon a user post that was one of the few posted by a woman to start a woman-focused discussion. It raised the question of whether hymen restoration surgery was *haram*.

The discussion was steeped with men's opinions, naturally. I'll be honest: clicking on it, I wasn't too eager to see the responses. Of course, most of the discussion was framed around the false notion of the hymen being a signifier of virginity and, thus, purity. I already knew how the conversation would go and even internalized it myself: *Of course she can't*, I thought to myself, a response conditioned by the patriarchal mentality that was all I had been exposed to. *That would be going against God's nature and be intentionally dishonest and misleading and whatnot.* But then, one comment by a Muslim woman stood out among the rest, like a light tower beckoning me home. This phenom of a woman thoughtfully said, "Islam gives equality to men and women, and that includes privacy. Since it is impossible to tell from a man's penis if he's had sex before, then women should be able to have that privacy as well."

Set aside the hypersexualization of the hymen as connected to virginity or any signifier of sexual activity, the assumption that a woman's sexuality is anyone else's business, the cultural and often religious connection of virginity with chastity, and our obsession with chastity as being a reflection of a woman's worth (and you would be crazy to think I'm just talking about Muslims, lest we forget every attorney's favorite go-to tactic of slut-shaming rape survivors). But, to me, reading that comment was like drinking from the chalice of liberation itself. Islamic interpretation had always, before then, seemed to me to be something that was exclusive to the learned men who spent years studying Muslim scholarship, who somehow possessed a greater authority to dictate our understanding of our religion with a reason that surpassed our own. The logic was that because they studied Islamic jurisprudence, they understood our religion better than anyone. But the thing is, that limitation automatically reserves Islamic interpretation to the most privileged facets of society: usually Arabic-speakers, usually affluent enough to attend higher institutions of learning, and usually men, whose viewpoints would inevitably be impacted by the patriarchal societies in which they were shaped. But, now, suddenly, I was reminded of the sheer accessibility of my religion—of our individual empowerment to use our God-given reason to determine for ourselves what our religion intended. That one comment opened up my mind to feminist interpretations of Islam, like I was at once introduced to the other side of the moon. I was hooked. There was another world out there, and it felt really, really good.

My next foray into feminist interpretation became the topic of wearing nail polish for *wudu*, or ablutions. The established opinion among our communities was that wearing nail polish during prayer was *haram* because it created a physical barrier preventing ablution water from touching your nails, thus making your ablution incomplete, and your *salaat*, or prayer, invalid. Truth be told, the five daily prayers obliged of Muslims were always a struggle for me throughout my life. It was so hard for me to commit to them, and one of the reasons why was because I was taught a very demanding criteria for my worship to be accepted. Muslim women not only had to make sure they weren't wearing nail polish or makeup (which could create a barrier from ablution water touching your face, or just straight-up make you look a hot mess when the water blurred your foundation or caused your eyeliner to run), but also they had to wear prayer clothes or otherwise be covered from head to toe and, as I was taught, had to be wearing a skirt or socks in order for prayers to count. The many gendered expectations placed on women to pray—when guys typically could just perform ablutions and drop down to their knees in *salaat* pretty much at any moment—almost made daily worship seem like a burden. Blasphemous, I know.

The nail polish thing was the biggest discouragement for me. In the back of my head, I always felt guilt like, *Okay, God has blessed me with so much and done so much for me—you're telling me, Amani, that you can't even be bothered to remove or sacrifice nail polish for Him?!* After my LiveJournal discovery, I was emboldened to find an alternative opinion on what seemed to be an obvious topic of contention for me. And I did. I stumbled upon an article published by a woman—a seemingly random lone blog post—in which she argued her own opinion that it should be okay for Muslim women to wear nail polish while performing ablutions. She posited that *wudu* is meant to be a spiritual cleanse more than a physical one, and if the woman is still performing ablutions with her nail polish on, it's not like she's skimping on any necessary rituals prior to prayer.

Prophet Muhammad, peace be upon him, even gave men who wore turbans at the time a pass during ablutions, suggesting they could simply wipe some water over their headpieces instead of completely unraveling and rewrapping them since that would be difficult and time-consuming. If our religion gave that much consideration to men's convenience regarding an ablution "barrier," you're telling me that women are not given that convenience regarding some nail polish, which has transformed into a gendered societal norm for many of us today? But then again, who were the ones issuing our *fatwas* and deciding on these interpretations that we were consuming? (Spoiler alert: men.) And if the whole point is praying to God, then wouldn't doing so with nail polish be better than not praying at all, instead of this zero-sum game imposed on women's spirituality?

It all suddenly made so much sense to me, and it was so liberating to see a regular Muslim woman exercise her right to logically interpret her religion for herself in a way that accommodated her gendered lifestyle. For the first time, I witnessed a compassionate interpretation of a contemporary issue for women that wasn't the harsh, unnecessarily difficult or strict opinion of a male authority about how we should practice. While Islam itself already granted many exceptions and privileges to women, especially when it comes to worship, this took Muslims' oft-repeated notion that men and women are "equal, but different" and flipped it on its head in undeniable favor of women.

I started to see the bigger picture of things: Islam was not relegated to the tiny, sometimes frustrating and seemingly arbitrary details of practice, but rather entered the larger picture of spirituality and worship that contextualized my womanhood. In order to be able to derive these logical conclusions about my religion, I had to go back to the basics and understand the very fundamental principles upon which it was founded: justice, social equality, racial equality, financial equality, and, possibly most important of all, gender equality. Thus began my lifelong love affair with Islamic feminism.

I craved more. The way Islamophobia squeezed me out of finding connections with my surroundings led me to searching for them online, seeking spaces for open and refreshing discourse that I couldn't have anywhere else. I remember stumbling upon a blog called Muslimah Media Watch,[1] one of the only websites of its kind at the time, which critically unpacked different portrayals of Muslim women in the media. It quickly became one of my favorites, and I felt it verbalized feelings that I'd always had but was never able to put my finger on. I acutely identified that I was leading a unique and trying experience as a millennial Muslim, the daughter of an immigrant and a refugee, born and raised in the United States—ostracized through bullying, heightened Islamophobia, and the difficult task of growing up as a young girl in a misogynistic and hypersexualized society. My life, and the lives of others like me, reflected a deeply entrenched double jeopardy to which Frances Beal first introduced us: the intersectional concept of being subjected to racism, and then further being subjected to sexism within that racist framework. While it refers to the unique and incomparable oppression of black women in the United States, Beal's concept of double jeopardy can unfortunately be applied in varying degrees to the exacerbation of many Muslim women's struggles in a post-9/11 era. Not only do we have to battle today's modern assault on our religion, but we also have to defy its sexist application to us both inside and outside of our own communities, all on top of the preexisting anti-black racism that black Muslim women suffer from Muslims and non-Muslims alike.

1 http://www.muslimahmediawatch.org/.

I knew that there *had* to be other girls who were going through these experiences, who also wanted to have conversations that were directly relevant to our Muslim lifestyles in today's society. I wanted to find them, and felt like there was no space online where we could connect. Most of the existing Muslim LiveJournal communities were inactive, or barely operating. The ones that were did not offer safe spaces for conversations that specifically centered on women. Of those that had large Muslim women memberships, the age group was either slightly or much older than my own, and not distinctly Western; thus the conversations were not always relatable to the distinct issues we were facing. So, given that I was already obsessed with LiveJournal and web design and coding layouts, and I felt this space was missing and we really needed it, I thought, *Why not?* I would make a new community entirely.

MuslimGirls is a place where you can ask those questions regarding Islam that you don't know who else to ask, where you can talk about random issues or girly topics that are a little too embarrassing for mom, where you can share articles that you find helpful or inspirational, where you can discuss current events regarding Muslims in the world, or simply where you can meet and get to know other Muslim girls online.

That was the first official mission statement that our teenage selves came up with in 2009. Within its first five days of going live, MuslimGirls garnered more than 1,000 new members. LiveJournal highlighted it on its homepage as an exciting new community to watch. Membership requests came flooding in, and what was most interesting to see was that many of them came from non-Muslims, eager to learn about our religion from fellow netizens to whom they could relate. The community was bustling with dozens of new member posts per day. The first few, posted by us moderators, were focused on hijab styles in addition to Islamic resources that we found useful to our lifestyles—like health tips that were taken from the Qur'an—and references for members unfamiliar with the basic tenets of Islam. As the community grew, it became flooded with users' questions, often about easy ways to implement or practice Islam in their daily lives. One post that started a lot of discussion early on was one member's confusion about the differences between Sunni and Shi'a Islam. We watched in awe as the community took on a life of its own. We could only assume it meant that we were cultivating something that many of us were yearning for.

Noticing that the increased attention also exposed us to more bigots, we stepped up our moderation and individually screened every single member request before accepting, in order to fiercely preserve the community as a safe space. At the time, we felt like Muslim girls were already experiencing so much abuse in the outside world that we wanted there to be one place online that could be our little haven. Many men were interested in joining and insisted they would just be flies on the wall—but, as the main post on the community stated, we rejected all requests from men in order to maintain a space exclusively for women and girls. After realizing that, wow, there was a real public interest here, and that Muslim girls wanted a platform like this and that others wanted to *learn* from a platform like this, I decided that it would be a good idea to move the conversation to its own website where it could be easily and publicly accessible. That's how Muslim Girl was born.

Years later, when one of our earliest bloggers and Maha's little sister, Sara, would see me on CNN debating Don Lemon and Alan Dershowitz, she would tell me that that was the vision we always had for Muslim Girl. That it would bring talking heads on the news that looked like us, speaking on our own behalf and leading the conversations that pertained to our lives. I'm not sure if there was ever an explicit moment when we knew Muslim Girl was going to become a cultural phenomenon. We knew the work that we were doing was important since day one, because we were filling a void and addressing a need that no one had identified yet but was so crucial to our lives. Our goal was always to increase our media representation and reclaim our narrative. And we always knew that if we were going to survive in today's society, there was no other option but to succeed.

Chapter 5

Muslim Girl's own coming of age took place in 2015, during what I will forever remember as the Summer of Hustle.

In May that year, I was packing up my apartment in Washington, DC, where I had moved straight out of college for a media relations job at the American-Arab Anti-Discrimination Committee. It was Faris's birthday. I had just completed my last day of work and officially resigned from the position that formed the foundation of my postgrad life, and was starting my first day at my dream job at Al Jazeera America in New York City in mere days. Uprooting the entire life I had started to establish for myself in DC was one of the most difficult decisions I had ever made, but the opportunity was one I felt it was worth dropping everything for.

While Baba was on his way down from New Jersey with a moving truck to help me pack my things, I received a call from Al Jazeera America's HR office in NYC.

"We need to postpone your start date," they said on the phone.

Naturally, I started freaking out. I was moving to Brooklyn *that day*, was suddenly unemployed, and expecting a ton of moving expenses. Now I'm suddenly hit with uncertainty about two whole weeks of salary—and maybe even my dream job altogether.

"You know, if you're nervous, it's not too late to undo all of this," Baba said. "You're still here. You can unpack your boxes. You can just go back to work tomorrow and tell them you changed your mind. You can stay here."

It wasn't until I graduated from Rutgers in 2014 and moved to DC that I decided to actively cultivate Muslim Girl as a publication. I developed a volunteer staff of editors and writers who were pure #MuslimGirlFire—a league of superwomen who were passionate about contributing to this labor of love for the sake of our collective benefit. We started shaping a regular publication schedule, storyboarding the contemporary topics we felt needed to be addressed, and got to igniting the conversation.

Prior to that, Muslim Girl had been a constant presence in my life and the lives of my friends, but it was always just a hobby for us. Interestingly enough, in that way, Muslim Girl grew up with us. When we got to college, we were introduced to feminist literature from titans such as bell hooks and Audre Lorde. In our archives, you can witness how the content on our site shifted from the daily musings of high school girls to more introspective criticisms of our lived experiences in the context of our society. That development continued postgrad as it sought new answers and experiences, inspiring new feminist analysis. In this way, Muslim Girl organically became a real-time chronicle of the evolution of our identities during one of the most pivotal moments in our modern history.

During this time, I was obsessively working on Muslim Girl like a second job. I'd wake up at mind-numbingly early hours of the morning to edit articles on the site before heading to work at nine a.m., then come straight home from work at five p.m. and continue developing Muslim Girl late into the night. When people asked, "Where is Muslim Girl based?" I'd jokingly respond, "Your nearest Wi-Fi hotspot." Just a scrappy blog, our hustle was coming at the world live from diners and coffee shops, anywhere with free internet and coffee refills. Digitally managing a team meant that borders melted away. It became like a virtual manifestation of badass superwomen taking on societal ills one blog post at a time, assembled through iMessage group chats and constant e-mail threads. Our initiative came with built-in sisterhood, and as we grew, so did our mentorship among one another; not only were we really cultivating a source of refuge for Muslim women online, but, in doing so, we also found it in each other. We were hooked.

It's during this time that our tagline became "Muslim Women Talk Back," because that's exactly what we chose to do. One of our first articles that went viral was about Mia Khalifa, the Christian Lebanese porn star whose most popular video featured her in nothing but a headscarf while performing sexual acts on a white guy. She had become one of the most popular porn stars on the internet that year, and blogs and news outlets were eager to paint Mia's story as one of women's empowerment and defiance against religion and culture. Of course, we had to disagree. Muslim Girl became one of the only sites to offer a critical analysis of Mia's success, garnered by what we argued was using a religious garment as a prop to portray colonial sexual fantasies. The article spread like wildfire and catapulted Muslim Girl to a new stratosphere, earning the attention of mainstream media outlets we otherwise never accessed.

Shortly after, our first major republication request came from *Fortune* magazine for an article on First Lady Michelle Obama's visit to Saudi Arabia, during which she chose not to cover her hair. This was not newsworthy anywhere in the world except America, apparently, where the media transformed her gesture into a grandiose statement for Saudi women's rights. Muslim Girl pushed back against the misconstrued coverage with an essay arguing that Saudi women have been organizing, mobilizing, and advocating for change in their society on their own without the need of any outsiders' help. The attention the essay received indicated to us that more and more people were interested in hearing what we had to say.

Muslim Girl reached even wider audiences a few months later when we decided to speak up against anti-Muslim bigot Pamela Geller's hatemongering. After the Charlie Hebdo massacre, she planned to host Draw Muhammad Day in Garland, Texas—an occasion for, I guess, other bigots to compete over who could draw the most offensive cartoon of our prophet for a cash prize, and then put all submissions on display in an art gallery. While never a justifiable incitement of violence, this was insulting to Muslims and our religion itself. But we figured the only way to talk back to such ridiculous hate would be with humor and love. So, we made a video in which we invited everyone to draw a Muhammad that they knew. Muhammad is the most common name in the world, after all, so we figured everyone must know a Muhammad! Our campaign effectively drowned out any negativity surrounding the event, heralded as a youthful and peaceful response to Islamophobia, and garnered us our first mention on *Time* magazine's website.

"I think I'm still going to go," I told Baba. "Everything happens for a reason. I'm sure everything will work out."

I didn't exactly realize the level of comfort and security I'd be leaving behind in that moment. The only clarity I had was that I felt a strong pull toward New York City that May. I felt that there was a reason life was taking me to one of the media capitals of the world, in spite of whether I consciously felt ready for it.

A few weeks later, I got a bleaker call from HR while enjoying a shish kebab dinner with my friend at my favorite restaurant in

Paterson, New Jersey. Al Jazeera America was postponing my start date again. At that moment, my friend could see that not even our kebab could keep me from the brink of tears.

"Listen, maybe it wasn't meant for you. Maybe the best thing is that you focus on Muslim Girl. I think you're supposed to be one of those amazing entrepreneurs. I think this moment is the hiccup in your story that changes everything."

Thus began the Summer of Hustle. I made the painful and terrifying decision to throw Al Jazeera America out the window, give everything I had to Muslim Girl for just one summer, and see what would come of it. I rented a cheap room in a brownstone apartment building deep in Bed-Stuy in the same neighborhood as Imam Siraj Wahhaj's congregation. I burned through all my savings from the past year in DC within two summer months to work on the website full-time. By the end of the summer, Muslim Girl had gone viral and landed its first major profile for the viewership it garnered.

The following summer, a video of comments I made during the White House's United State of Women Summit went viral on social media. My voice was being given a platform as a speaker at the summit alongside media titans like Oprah Winfrey, Meryl Streep, and Tina Fey, along with the most powerful women in our government. When we were taping the commercial film that would end up covered in every major news outlet on the entire planet, dubbing us "Michelle Obama's Kick-Ass Lady Crew," I was sitting in the VP of marketing's office in the PepsiCo headquarters in Manhattan, staring at a moving camera and a crew of filmmakers.

"She has such powerful eyes," one of them said. "Shoot a close-up of her eyes the way that we did earlier for Shonda Rhimes. Give her the Shonda Rhimes treatment."

What? Shonda Rhimes?

The day of the summit, I was seated between Shonda Rhimes and Gloria Steinem on a panel about media representation, and we spoke about diversity. I suggested that it's crucial for us to keep representation in mind when we think about who's included in the process. I was referring to the case of Hollywood employing white actors to play positive minority roles, while brown actors are relegated to negative roles perpetuating racist depictions.

During the summer of 2016 I also traveled to France for the first time to attend the Cannes Lions International Festival of Creativity. I was the sole visibly Muslim woman speaker invited to speak on the main stage among the global makers and shakers of the industry. It wasn't until the chief creative officer of the ad agency that had invited me there referred to it as the "Oscars of the media world" that I realized just how big of a deal this was. It was a milestone. Because Muslim women haven't had a presence in a space that pretty much dictates the way we perceive the world around us, it's no wonder our misrepresentation has gotten this bad. If media is the ultimate lens through which we distort our views of different people—which, as I learned early on, could perpetuate harmful misconceptions as fodder for war—then this is one of the most potent avenues of getting at the root.

Now that I'm being exposed to the culture of who's running our ad and media world, I could say the same for this space. When I was walking through the Palais des Festivals, I stopped at the wall on which the names and photos of award nominees that year were exhibited. Of the few categories highlighted, not only were women scarce, but I didn't see the name of one single black person. When we consider this, it becomes easier to understand how our media simply does not look like the world around us. The people included in the process are not representative of the marginalized people who would most benefit from more accurate and positive depictions of them.

During my visit to France, the UK voted on seceding from the European Union—to #Brexit—and won. My British hosts were heartbroken, stunned that the unimaginable had suddenly, overnight, become reality. The morning after the decision came, we met up in the *Guardian*'s speakers' lounge to prepare for a rehearsal. The idea of Brexit passing seemed so unlikely that our organizers were visibly moved, with a somber pall of confusion washing over everyone as they attempted to comprehend what country they'd be returning to. They were from London, which had voted to remain, along with Scotland and Northern Ireland. "I just didn't think it could ever actually happen," they kept repeating.

The campaign to Brexit was not unlike that of Donald Trump. Both used fallacies about immigrants and the refugee crisis to illustrate a racist idea that our collective identity has been manipulated by minorities entering our borders. This idea echoes familiar age-old notions of racial purity. Trump has especially homed in on ostracizing the Muslim community as a central part of his platform, such as by asserting that the San Bernardino shooters were only able to commit their heinous act "because we let their families" into our country. Further, the Brexit campaign just as stupidly assumed that a supposed solution as simple as leaving the EU would fix the economy. In the U.S., Trump was touting the mind-numbing suggestion that we erect a physical wall between the U.S. and Mexico. And in both of our great nations, nobody had been heeding any warning of the consequences that would result from either outcome.

Not everyone felt the same way though. Walking through the

festival, a British duo pointed at me, for some strange reason, and cheerfully exclaimed, "We're not part of the EU anymore!" I can only assume it was a celebratory announcement that they wouldn't have to deal with people like me anymore. I immediately flashed back to the tensions we were witnessing in the United States as a result of our own issues with race. While I was experiencing this historic development in Europe, across the pond my newsfeed back in the U.S. was flooded with shock, and, even more, with fear. As the East Coast woke to a different world, thought pieces started pouring out about the parallels between the Brexit referendum and the rise of Donald Trump, and one reality was staring us in the face: As impossible as we were hoping—imagining—the rise of racism to be, it can, in fact, win. The UK's decision was a clear demonstration of that, and, at worst, it was a sign of what was waiting for us come November.

In response to Brexit, Trump said, "I hope America is watching." Watching what, exactly? Maybe the tragic spectacle that exploiting racism among racists for a national campaign, that otherwise would have no standing, works.

Within three days after the vote, the Muslim Council of Britain had recorded 100 Islamophobic incidents. The British National Police Chiefs' Council noted a 57 percent increase in reported hate crimes, with 337 total by the end of the week. A video went viral on social media in the days following the vote, showing white teens on a Manchester bus verbally attacking a military veteran of color and telling him to "go back to Africa!" At the same time as the Brexit campaign amplified racism against immigrants entering the country, it also drew on resentment toward Syrian refugees by suggesting that their entry would put British women at risk of sexual assault. The latter reiterates the traditional British colonial inference that its white women were superior objects of desire to uncontrollable and inherently devious brown men that, today, the UK was in danger of having wash up on its shores. The tragic irony is that the wealth that the UK sought to protect with #Brexit was robbed from the home countries of many of its immigrants, and the refugee crisis is the result of political complacency that has now been coming home to roost.

It seemed to me that the Brits around me were suddenly confronted by the stark reality of their makeup, a truthful reminder of their nation's racist history that, even in 2016, the country just couldn't seem to shake off. I imagine it's how we Americans felt when we somberly watched the poll numbers rise in favor of Donald Trump, when we introspectively watched during the primaries as states, one by one, like dominoes, bolstered his rise. I fear the feeling I will have when the same thing happens as states flip to red in favor of Trump during election night. For us Americans, it has been an avalanche, something uncontrollable, something deeply revealing of the psyche of our country. At the very least, we've seen it coming. It's been measured symptomatically for months. For the UK, the thought was so far gone that they never really imagined it happening. Self-aware as they were, many expected the numbers to be close, but none—even those who voted to leave—ever really foresaw it. The racism was supposed to stay politely tucked away within homes and at dinner tables.

Chapter 6

"The media is hype about Muslim women right now, but only the ones that fit a certain kind of image," I told Contessa. I was finishing up my makeup in the studio bathroom as she taped more of our conversation for the CNN reel.

It's so meta. You have to wear a headscarf, of course, because the media's lazy perception of Muslim women—and the only visual they're keen to perpetuate—is that all of them wear headscarves. Plus, the Muslim community can more easily see you as a woman leader if you satisfy this requirement. That's the qualifier. Then, after that, you have to be some level of attractive, of course. In societal terms, that means a lighter complexion is a major bonus. That privilege has been on my mind a lot this year: If I was a Muslim woman with darker skin, maybe a chocolate color rather than the honey-caramel flavor that was acceptable for being not too foreign but just enough, then I doubt I'd be getting as much airtime as I am right now. Maybe not nearly as many people would care about hearing what I have to say.

Then, of course, you have to be fashion-forward. Like, you need to wear a headscarf and show that you're still different, but you need to make them forget that you're different by mixing it with the perfect combination of Western trends to remind everyone that you're also the same. It has to be a testament to our country's obsession with the way women dress: Even when the outward intent of media attention on Muslim women is inclusivity, the extent of it has gotten stuck on our presumably outrageous ability to dress modestly and with good taste—according to our society's standard—at the same time. "Muslim Women Push Back Against Stereotypes!" was the hot headline in varying degrees—the story was always about the way we dress. Not, for example, our activism, our business acumen, our personal success. Before Muslim Girl started consciously reshifting the attention of the media, recentering the actual Muslim women whether they were behind headscarves or not, for a good amount of time the headscarves were the story. The narrative was exclusionary and always centered around how we are able to make moves *in spite of* a marker on our heads, or, possibly even worse, *because* of it. There is a renewed sense of animosity among some within the Muslim community whenever a new story goes viral of a Muslim woman that wants to be "the first hijabi _____"—fill in the blank with preferred career, profession, or vocation.

When this trend started taking off in the media a few years ago, it spurred criticisms of self-tokenization. The catch is that a lot of the time, when you're a (visible) minority who is among the first to make progress in new spaces, your presence will be tokenized. The hope is that this temporary state dissolves as more and more of us enter these spaces along our evolving strides in representation. One thing that gets neglected from the conversation is that often, tokenization is a means of survival of its own. It can take cards that have been unevenly dealt against us, that by any other means would be used to suppress our livelihoods, and subversively transform them into a brief moment of opportunity to reshuffle the deck. This happens on a large scale when tokenized peoples use their acquired privileges to push the collective further.

More often than not, tokenization is forcefully imposed on us, and not just on an individual level, but on a community level as well. When all the public eye sees are headscarves instead of individual stories, our community is collectively tokenized. It creates the perception that opportunity is limited and only a rare few of us can make it. Whenever that happens to an already marginalized community, it pits its own members in a competition against one another instead of against the restrictive frameworks that put us in that position in the first place. The first hijabi whatever won't eliminate Islamophobia just as the first black president hasn't eliminated racism, though both are signifiers of some type of progress—symbols of ascending beyond adversity.

When we get tokenized for our identities, the single story that Chimamanda warned us about easily happens. One Muslim woman's story is taken to represent Muslim women like a monolith, like an absolute truth that exists for all of us. The intricacies of the different identities that exist among Muslim women far beyond their faith are melted away. One question that Muslim Girl often struggles with is that of our representation of Muslim women and their diverse struggles in other parts of the world. The truth is that Muslim women come from literally every walk of life, and being fully aware of our own Western privilege, we cannot possibly attempt to speak on their behalf. However, our privilege affords us influence that many women in other parts of the world do not possess. When we do not have the opportunity to uplift them into these spaces, the best that we can do is use our unique position to create an impact that we hope will ripple out. This is the premise upon which Muslim Girl was founded. Knowing that failed domestic and foreign policy has fallen on the mischaracterization of the Muslim woman's narrative, reclaiming it would alter the public's perception of our needs and opinions and cultivate a stronger presence for us in the public sphere. When that happens, especially as residents of the primary exporter of failed foreign policy in the Muslim world, we wield power to change policies that directly impact the lives of women abroad. We can never speak on their behalf or have our single stories represent their struggles, but what we can do is attempt to use our privileges to make radical change.

I look back at my reflection. A part of me resents the light-colored contacts I wear: an abstract mix between periwinkle blue and seafoam green, framed by the dark, thick eyebrows that my classmates would chastise me for in school and the black Middle Eastern lashes that my elementary school nurse once told me I should have thinned out, because they were too much.

At the same time, these light attributes have become colonized as Western standards of beauty. The high demands of the media world create intense pressure to cater to and unrealistically live up to them. The racial undertones are palpable. With brown eyes, I'm Arab. With gray eyes, I'm exotic, racially ambiguous. With my contacts in, people ask me where I'm from out of admiration. Without them, people ask me where I'm from because I look too different to possibly be from here.

"You can talk, but you also have the look," a producer told me once. I could tell she hesitated so as to not offend me. It's no surprise to me that appearance is often the gatekeeper. In my case, my media-standard look has garnered me access to spaces and people to which I would otherwise be denied. They've given my voice and what I have to offer a vessel through which people might give a second listen to what I have to say, as sad as it is that people might barely pay attention otherwise.

———

I still feel intense pressures regarding my body image, despite having lost a hundred pounds in a year. I've always felt indescribable pressure to lose weight, become smaller, less in the way. My weight loss reminded me of declawing a feline. The woman shrinks, she takes up less room, her body makes everyone else in the room more comfortable. And, no, it's not always about health. Even at my highest weight, my doctor told me that my health was the ideal profile for anyone my age. I was just as awesome at my heaviest. But when I became lighter, people finally began to see me—just for the wrong reasons.

"Sometimes you have to play the game to change the game," I admit to Contessa. Play the system so you can share the stage with Bill Clinton and then mention the Boycott, Divestment, and Sanctions movement. Deal the cards right so you can get invited to speak at a White House summit and then remind the audience that our government drones Muslim girls like you in other parts of the world. That's what privilege looks like.

The bathroom conversation never made it into the final cut. The featured image for the CNN profile was a landscape close-up frame of my eyes.

I was part of the opening plenary of Clinton Global Initiative University (CGI U) at University of California, Berkeley—the very first panel to kick off the entire event—and it was moderated by former president Bill Clinton himself. My co-panelists included NASA astronaut Cady Coleman, Pinterest founder Ben Silbermann, Khan Academy founder Salman Khan, and "We are all Khaled Said" Facebook page founder Wael Ghonim. It was such an honor to be sitting among them. When I first met Wael in the holding room before our panel was to begin, I immediately flashed back to the hundreds of pages of research I did in college that were inspired by his Facebook page and the developments of the revolution it sparked. The Tunisian and Egyptian revolutions took place just as I had started college, so you can imagine the powerful impact they had on my outlook of our generation during one of the most important transitions in a young American adult's life. To me, nothing was impossible. There were no limits to what we could accomplish together. Commence the many moments of activism that breathed life into me at Rutgers University, from organizing for Palestinian human rights, to taking on censorship at the *Daily Targum*, the Rutgers University daily newspaper, to eventually occupying an administrative building and ousting former secretary of state Condoleezza Rice from speaking at our 2014 commencement. But I digress.

When we all took our seats on stage beneath the blinding blue lights at CGI U, I realized that I was the last panelist—and the one sitting directly beside Bill Clinton. I was stunned by my positioning and quickly conferred that it had to be for the photo ops. Super bonus points for a former president to be gracious and inclusive enough to have a hijabi on his stage. In fact, three out of the five of us were Muslims, and I hardly think that was a coincidence. Hillary Clinton was in a tight race against Bernie Sanders, and he was getting major social justice points. He was the progressive king at the moment. Only a few weeks ago, Hillary had been at the annual American Israel Public Affairs Committee convention—and she'd given a hawkish speech about the need to support Israel's right to self-defense at all costs. In American terms, that meant killing unarmed and defenseless civilians. When I first contemplated the speaking invitation from the Clinton Foundation, I called up my friend and Muslim badass Laila Abdelaziz, an employee at the Council on American-Islamic Relations in Tampa, Florida. I expressed my concerns to her about accepting an invite from the foundation given the current political climate.

"OH MY GOD, you HAVE to go!" she exclaimed. "Amani, you HAVE to. That is SUCH a platform. Who cares what people think? Just go and say what you have to say," she said on the phone. Not gonna lie, maybe my own butterflies had something to do with it. I told her I was kind of nervous, and scared I wouldn't make the best use of the opportunity.

"Yeah, I will tell you," she started, "I was invited to a closed-door meeting with Hillary, and I accepted it SOLELY because I wanted to use the opportunity to talk to her about BDS." She was referring to the Boycott, Divestment, and Sanctions movement—a nonviolent civil response to Israel's international law violations. It's a movement modeled off of the humanitarian response to the South African apartheid regime, which was the only non-military response in history that ever successfully defeated apartheid. "When she was right in front of me, and she was shaking my hand, I completely froze. They are VERY intimidating," she said. Crap. Now I was even more nervous.

At CGI U, Bill Clinton welcomed the summit and then opened up our plenary session by posing a statement to me that would later play back on GIFs and memes across the Internet: "This is a pretty steep career lens for a Muslim woman," he said.

In that moment, I really didn't have time to think of how to gingerly word my reply or consider how respectable it would sound when I responded. "I actually don't think it is too steep for a Muslim woman."

My response was met with several moments of raucous applause from the woke San Francisco student audience. In those brief seconds, I was merely reacting to a latent offense I felt at his words. "For a Muslim woman." That phrase alone encapsulates much of how the media has been treating stories of Muslim women over the past two years or so. It's interesting because on the outside, it seems like Muslim women are gaining a lot of inclusion, but are we really? You might have noticed that likely much of the positive media attention that you've encountered that has been focused on Muslim women has treated them as exceptional subjects due to their religion. "Why this Muslim woman is breaking stereotypes [insert something mediocre here]."

This is not to negate the incredible work and accomplishments of Muslim women; on the contrary, it's important for us to recognize that those works and accomplishments deserve recognition in their own right—not solely because they were produced by a Muslim woman. That's not what makes them valuable. To assert so is to imply that, inversely, Muslim women are *unlikely* to do x, y, and z. Muslim women are uniquely incapable of doing this. The only thing that makes their work special is that it's done by a woman whom we would otherwise presume to be prevented from doing so, because she is oppressed, or uneducated, or weak, and her success is something of an anomaly. While it's welcome to celebrate the accomplishments of Muslim women *in spite* of societal challenges, only framing their stories in this way continues to center the status quo. The story becomes not about the hard work to which she has dedicated herself, but ironically about the hurdles in place to prevent her from doing it.

Worse still is when this framing forces a preconstructed narrative of the Muslim woman's lived experience. For example, I had an experience with a major publication that took my story of how I am defying cultural norms through my personal choices and twisted it into a #basic and offensive story portraying me as rebelling against my religion itself. It was manufactured to be your run-of-the-mill "poor Muslim girl restricted by Islam and trying to break free" type of anecdote by intentionally washing away the nuance of my personal account. Sure, we can play the system to get our message and our voices out there, but we must also beware getting played the heck out in the media's rapid commodification of the headscarf and Muslim women as a hot headline for hits, views, or sales.

When it comes to Muslim women, the public wants a superhero to consume. We are praised when we are badasses who talk back. Our headscarves are imagined to really be condensed capes. We are cheered through Facebook likes and Instagram hearts when we stand up to society in various ways, as if we are not vulnerable, have nothing to lose, or are not putting our lives on the line by doing so.

I wrote a Facebook status during the height of what I'm going to start referring to as the Trump Scare, after he made those horrible Muslim-ban comments, about a terrifying moment on NJ Transit when I found myself to be the only woman left in my train car. A man walked up to me, physically put his hands on my scarf, and asked, "Are you going to let me take this off of you later?"

Everyone commenting on my Facebook status was eager to hear how the story played out. Did I tell him off? What did I say? How did he respond? How did it end? I guess we somewhat have the double-edged sword of the internet and social media to thank for desensitizing us and reducing precarious life events into two-dimensional fodder for entertainment. But then one commenter disrupted the pattern.

"I really don't understand how everyone is responding with such amusement, as if Amani didn't just describe an obviously dangerous situation," she said. "How about we all stop pretending this is some fairy-tale wet dream about a superhero hijabi who breaks all stereotypes and tears things up?"

Chapter 7

Here are the rough, general, immediate guidelines as to how Muslims react whenever a public act of violence takes place: 1) Pray to God that the perp is not Muslim. Dear God, spare us this one. Please. 2) Compulsively follow any convenient corporate news outlet or subsequent trending hashtag on developments, oscillating between mourning the victims and fearing for the sanctity of your life. 3) If the perp is identified to be white and/or non-Muslim, emotionally prepare yourself for the trauma of having the double standard dangled in your face again that they are just "mentally disturbed," because, remember, the word *terrorism* only applies to people that are shades of brown. 4) If they're identified as Muslim and then inevitably as a terrorist, or having ties to some terrorist organization, or, even more conveniently, as having outwardly proclaimed loyalty to a terrorist group somehow, mentally prepare for the—possibly violent—backlash. 5) In the case of our highly digital Muslim community, prepare a corresponding Facebook status: whether offering thoughts and prayers for the respective Western city, exasperation at the hypocritical label of a "lone white shooter," or an urgent and woeful reminder that all Muslim and "Muslim-passing" friends stay safe in the ensuing media frenzy of another terrorist attack.

The mistreatment of the definition of terrorism—did you know the United Nations doesn't even have an established definition of what it is? But the U.S. sure does, and it's quite an exclusive and broad one all at the same time—really skews people's perceptions of Muslims and the atrocities taking place around the world.

In the summer of 2016, MTV aired a new web show with me on the issues that impact Muslim Americans on their Snapchat Discover channel to millions of viewers, an episode of which listed several of my recent and ridiculous encounters with the Transportation Security Agency. They were pretty tragic cases of racial profiling, but spun to be hilarious and understandable to the network's preteen audience. I'm all for packaging an otherwise marginalized message in a way that will be digestible to its recipients—hey, that's what Prophet Muhammad did, wasn't it? One Snapchat user responded to the TSA episode by saying, "Instead of complaining about things we need to do to be safe, how about you talk about how terrorists should stop killing people." While I usually ignored such inquiries without even batting an eyelash, I took the bait and engaged, maybe because of how deep the stupidity of his comments hit a nerve.

I replied to this dude with a data plan and social media access and thus opinions worth sharing with, "Racial profiling people at airport security is actually a detriment to our safety. Think about it—there could be a white person passing through a gate with a bomb on him because we didn't search him properly, because TSA was too busy being fixated on people that look like me." As I was leaving the Nice airport after the Cannes Lions festival, I passed through the security machine, and it didn't even beep, but the French National Police still stopped me for an additional search. They gave me a very invasive and public pat down, cupping my boobs and butt, hands too close for comfort in my groin area, straight down to the bottom soles of my shoes to check for a bomb. It was humiliating. The white girl behind me passed through and actually set off the detector beeping, and she was let through without any additional inconvenience.

He responded, "No one else is killing innocent people like Muslims!"

"It's easy to think that way," I Snapchatted him back. "What happens is that whenever Muslims do something wrong, they are always in the news and identified as their religion. When people of other faiths commit horrible acts, we are never told what religion they are because it's deemed irrelevant, and they get to enjoy the privilege of being held accountable as individuals for their actions rather than having their background be collectively held accountable or blamed on their behalf.

"The term 'terrorism' is only ever applied to Muslims, but never when it's people of other faiths. Like the KKK, Christian conservatives that bomb abortion clinics, etc.," I continued. In this way, it's easy to see how the public garners a skewed perception of Muslims and Islam. Zoom in on the fringe minority of any group— rather than, in this case, the 1.6 billion[1] majority of all the other Muslims in the world that come from all walks of life and live peacefully in their societies (if Islam was really founded on terrorism, imagine the havoc of 1.6 billion terrorists in the world? Or even just half that many? *Allahu akbar*, for real.)—and *obviously* that would create a super limited and distorted image of a people. Like, imagine if we only focused on racists like Dylann Roof and said that's what all white people are like? Imagine if I demanded

1 Bill Chapell, "World's Muslim Population Will Surpass Christians This Century, Pew Says," NPR, April 2, 2015, http://www.npr.org/sections/thetwo-way/2015/04/02/397042004/muslim -population-will-surpass-christians-this-century-pew-says.

an apology from my local Starbucks barista for the racial slur her white peer hurled at me from his car window as I walked into the store? Would that make any sense at all? Of course not.

This, my friends, is how you manufacture hate.

Before Trump's inexcusable comments about inciting a ban on all Muslims, the sharpest I had felt this phenomenon since 9/11 was on the day that the Boston Marathon bombers were identified. I was interning for Vice in New York at the time. It was my first editorial internship, hard-fought for and hard-won. I discovered the Vice internships well past the term deadline, calling their office, and asking if I could still send in an application. "All the positions have been filled," the secretary told me. I sent in a Hail Mary email to the main contact anyway, insisting that their current representation of Muslim narratives—limited to only Michael Muhammad Knight at the time—did not offer enough of a voice for their Muslim audience, which I surely could bring to the table. I remember how elated I was when I got the call, and how I pranced around my newsroom at the *Daily Targum*, where I had been elected as opinions editor that year, to my peers' congratulations at the news. I got a coveted Vice internship.

That morning, I was getting ready to commute from New Brunswick, New Jersey, to the Vice headquarters in Williamsburg, Brooklyn, when the news of the Boston bombers' Muslim faith broke. For Muslims, the media victimizes all 1.6 billion of us with each news cycle. This became blatant in the case of the shooting of Pulse nightclub in Orlando, Florida, in June 2016. When the shooter's name was revealed to sound Muslim, the media immediately announced the shooting as a terrorist attack; perpetuated unsubstantiated claims of a proclamation to ISIS, or Al Qaeda, or Hezbollah, one of those; and placed the spotlight on a Muslim immigrant father and the narrative of a seemingly "foreign" family, suddenly forgetting that mass shootings are as American as apple pie.[2] It conveniently neglected that over 70 percent of mass shootings on our soil have been committed by white men—and that, if we were to follow #TrumpLogic, we are rightfully entitled to profile and denounce all white men, and possibly ban them from our country, given this information. No. Now, anti-gay sentiment was decentered as the issue, and what broke my heart the most was that many of the people around me fell into this trap. "It was certainly, without a doubt, connected to Islam," a haughty white agnostic investor explained to me over freshly squeezed lemonade in the East Village one sweltering afternoon in New York. "No, I mean, this was definitely about the Muslim religion," a gay Jewish white male colleague told me during our trip in France, after I sighed to him about how exhausted I was by the public overlooking this incident as a violent outburst of homophobia. The LGBTQA+ community was doing a noble job of defying Islamophobia during such a sensitive time that I had expected to find an ally in him. Did you notice that almost all the people insisting they are experts on Islam and that perpetuate the most inaccurate notions of Muslims like they are facts are always non-Muslims?

So, on that otherwise usual morning heading to my Vice internship, when the Boston bombers were identified as Muslim, I hit the brakes on everything. I was literally *out the door*, but then stopped dead in my tracks and retreated to a chair in my living room, hovered there for what seemed like an eternity, and whipped out my phone to get some friends' input while I calcu-

2 http://www.cnn.com/2016/06/12/us/orlando-nightclub-shooting/.

lated the severity of the situation. The first person I texted was a photographer friend that had been working in the city for years after he graduated from our alma mater.

"Hey, did you hear? They're Muslim," I said.

"Yea," he texted back.

"I'm honestly too scared to go to the Vice office today. I can't ride the subway!!!! What if someone pushes me onto the tracks or something? NY is going to be hell today," I spilled.

"If you're scared, they win," he responded.

So I went to Vice that day.

After what honestly felt like a harrowing trek to Brooklyn, my self-awareness on 100 and my alertness to my surroundings even higher than that, I finally found my way into the office safely and trudged over to my desk beside the rest of the interns, tossing my heavy bag in front of me with a sigh of relief. I probably wasn't in my chair for a good five minutes before the intern beside me—the carefree one that I'd had orientation with, who at the time had been really excited about the flowing booze he would soon enjoy at Vice parties almost as much as the non-traditional work environment we were entering with hippo-sized rhinestone-embellished panties on the wall—swiveled over to my side with his laptop in his hands.

"Hey, Amani," he said, "you're Muslim, right? Do you mind taking a look at these Qur'an verses and searching for anything that could hint at why the Boston bombers did what they did?"

It sucks that Muslims don't get some type of trigger warning just for being exposed to extreme anti-Muslim bigotry in our society. I've always wanted to do the research on how much of an emotional toll today's climate takes on Muslim youth. I know that for Palestinians, whenever a major assault is taking place in Palestine overseas, my young Palestinian American peers here often experience a sweeping depression, sometimes even physical illness.

It is mentally, emotionally, and physically exhausting to have to assert your humanity time and time again. It is exhausting to have to denounce violent actions on behalf of your entire religion, and then be subject to hideous moments like these.

"Um, I really don't think Qur'an verses had anything to do with their actions," I told him. "They were crazy."

"Yeah, yeah," he said. "Could you take a look at them anyway?"

Several weeks earlier, as I got into the swing of things in my semester-long internship, I found Vice editor in chief Rocco Castoro sitting at his desk. I made a coffee run as my excuse to pass by him, hovering at the coffee machine as I mustered up the courage to walk up to him. Then I did it. I went up to him, introduced myself, and said, "I want a Vice column."

Startled at first, he asked me what I had in mind, and I told him how I felt like having a space on Vice would give my voice as a Muslim woman a groundbreaking platform on political and social issues. He chewed on the idea a bit, thought it was cool, and referred me to the Features Editor Who Made These Decisions. As I turned to walk away, he stopped me.

"Wait a minute," he said. "I want to get your opinion on something."

I turned back, excited and flattered that my input was going to be used on something important enough to be on Rocco's desk. I was the only veiled Muslim woman in the newsroom and it was cute how much my college self freaking admired Vice. I wouldn't have been able to imagine that a few short years later, Muslim Girl would become the first Muslim website to partner with them in their influential ad network.

"We're deciding on the cover for the next issue of *Vice* magazine," he said. "It's the Hate Issue. I'm deciding between these two options—what do you think?" He pulled out two print versions of the cover and laid them in front of me.

On the left, there was a makeshift *Vice* cover with a photo of the KKK burning a cross. On the right, there was another mock cover, this one with an image I was much more familiar with, but that was still completely foreign to me: It was a photo of a brown man with a military vest on, wearing a green headband with the Islamic proclamation of faith wrapped around his head, against the backdrop of some conflict zone with a dead bleeding body and a rampaging fire behind him. He was holding up soldiers' dog tags in his hands and had an assault rifle in his lap.

"I think you should go with the KKK one," I told him, after a few moments of silence. He might have thought I was thinking it over, but really I was trying to calm my panicking thoughts that even Vice would betray me like this. "I think the picture of the Muslim guy is a really stereotypical depiction that already exists all over the media. It just reaffirms this skewed image of Muslims. But the KKK one, for the Hate Issue, would be interesting, because that's the type of imagery that people need to be reminded of, and it's not common. It would be different."

He looked at the two covers and back up at me, surveying

my reaction. "Hm, that's very interesting," he said. "All right, thank you."

After an exhausting day at the Vice office dealing with the Boston bombing coverage and Intern Who Just Doesn't Get It, I threw my heavy bag over my shoulder again, carrying the Macbook Pro I had been lugging around on my commute for this internship for months. As I was walking out, I passed by the reception desk, and something caught my eye. I stopped, and it was a stack of printed copies of the new Hate Issue. The cover staring back at me was of the brown man with the military vest. I walked out of the office's glass double doors and didn't return to my internship again.

The winter of 2015 was a tumultuous and difficult one to navigate. The second Paris attack of the year had just taken place in November, and the Muslim American community was still dealing with imminent backlash as a result of the sensational media coverage when the San Bernardino shooting happened only a few weeks later. The oncoming confusion with all the mixed information surrounding the shooters came to a head when the *New York Post* published a cover photo of San Bernardino victims with the large overset headline MUSLIM KILLERS. The irresponsible journalism and hysterical, propagandized coverage wildly legitimized anti-Muslim sentiment and made leaving our homes all the more difficult.

The aftermath brought with it a series of attacks on the Muslim American community in rapid, head-spinning succession. In Seattle, a Somali teenager was beaten and thrown off the roof of a six-story building. Bigots shot at a Muslim woman as she was leaving a mosque in Tampa. A little sixth-grade girl was taunted with the name "ISIS" as her boy classmates in the Bronx ripped the scarf off of her head and physically beat her on the playground. Two days after Trump's call for a Muslim ban, our team at Muslim Girl felt compelled to publish a "Crisis Safety Manual for Muslim Women" for basic survival in the aftermath of the San Bernardino shooting. I started distancing myself from social media at this time, lessening the log-ins and the amount of posts—only staying plugged in long enough to stay informed for our Muslim Girl coverage. Unfortunately, there were no trigger warnings for "vilifying you for your religion," "subjugation & dehumanization," or "delegitimizing your existence."

As a veiled Muslim woman, I was yet again overcome with a fear of leaving my house in the morning. The type of rhetoric Trump was using—banning all Muslims from the country, like we were different, incompatible with American life, like we didn't belong—made even a born and raised Jersey girl like me feel like an outsider all over again. I was frustrated, because I had already been through this before. I already lived through and survived this assault on my identity. And as a society, we're supposed to be progressing forward, not backward. The Muslim community worked tirelessly against this type of hatred since 2001, and suddenly, like a slippery slope, Trump had us falling right back down to where we started. The thought that another generation of little girls would have to endure an experience that almost broke me, that was the most difficult thing in my life to navigate, was truly heartbreaking. And so Muslim Girl decided that this time, instead of wasting space on our platform to talk back to Donald Trump—engaging in the same broken-record disputes and responding to the same unfair attacks on our humanity that we have collectively been facing since 9/11—we would stop giving Trump any space on our platform at all. He didn't deserve it, and we deserved better.

It was during this time that I started actively pitching Muslim Girl so that we could sustain our increasingly critical work. *The Harvard Law Review* published Nancy Leong's analysis on racial capitalism in June 2013, which analyzes "the process of deriving social and economic value from the racial identity of another person." While we were dishing out Muslim Girl's neatly streamlined numbers in pretty PowerPoint slides at shiny conference tables, trying to quantify and convince in dollar signs why Muslim women's voices are valuable, all I could really think about was how our site had to resort to publishing a crisis safety manual for Muslim women just to live. All the hateful rhetoric in the media—Paris, San Bernardino, now Trump—wasn't made in a void. The social complacency that Muslim Girl was created to combat has real life or death consequences for Muslim women in Western societies. While the world scapegoats Islam, Muslim women quickly become the most vulnerable targets, and, yet, the fashion industry and corporations are simultaneously eager to profit off of them.

At the same time, 2015 saw the trending topic of modest fashion and a huge surge of interest in Muslim women as consumers. Leong argues that "nonwhiteness has acquired a unique value because, in many contexts, it signals the presence of the prized characteristic of diversity," yet warns that "the 'thin' version of the diversity objective—emphasizes numbers and appearances. That is, it is exclusively concerned with improving the superficial appearance of diversity."[3] This can be said of many of the media outlets cashing in on hijab headlines while maintaining often racially or religiously uniform newsrooms, but also of the fashion industry's treatment of modest fashion. Many brands, from DKNY to Dolce & Gabbana, started launching their own modest fashion lines catered to Muslim women. Global media outlets heralded H&M for including a headscarf-clad model in their marketing campaign. Yet few brands have successfully integrated Muslim women fashion designers, consultants, or models into their lines, nor have they championed causes that would benefit the women from whom they'd gain the profit. In this way, what would otherwise appear to be a positive step in social inclusivity could have adverse effects on Muslim women, by putting out of business the designers that have been creating headscarves and abayas long before they became an Instagram sensation.

And then there's this question: In the midst of the severe backlash and threat against Muslim women's bodies, how many companies claiming to represent Muslim women actually made statements in support of them? How many blogs celebrating modest fashion also covered our stories of discrimination?

Muslim women are hot right now. The thing is, we can't be cool with society vilifying our identities while at the same time trying to profit off them. One thing became clear: Muslim Girl became a start-up because it had to. For us, entrepreneurialism is a means to an end. It's survival.

On top of all this, law enforcement and the media are usually slow to consider obviously biased incidents as hate crimes.

3 Nancy Leong, "Racial Capitalism," *Harvard Law Review*, June 2013, 2152, 2169, http://harvardlawreview.org/wp-content/uploads/pdfs/vol126_leong.pdf.

This results in frequent media misrepresentation of the severity of anti-Muslim bigotry, which has a profound negative effect on our community, especially on those Muslim women by whom they are so fascinated. Yusor Abu-Salha was shot execution-style in her Chapel Hill, North Carolina, apartment in February 2015, along with her husband and little sister. The murders, committed by their angry and admittedly anti-religion neighbor, were dismissed in the media far and wide as simply being "a parking dispute." It pains me to think that people would have been more interested in how Yusor styled her scarf than in what caused the senseless violence that took her life.

Trump discovered that milking anti-Muslim sentiment, with complete disregard to the dangers it poses to our very lives, keeps him in the spotlight and gets him more airtime. Since his ascension to the national stage, I have been receiving press requests around the clock during his media circuses to explain, again and again, "the current climate for Muslim women." By the time the Muslim-ban comments came, I had run out of different palatable ways to say, "Our lives are under threat right now"—ironically, not from ISIS extremism or the brown men that our society is raising pitch forks against, but from our own Western society itself.

Amid all the chaos, I witnessed one interesting development for the first time in my entire life since 9/11. When Trump's words rang around the country, many Americans were roused to rise to the defense of their Muslim neighbors. Social and broadcast media highlighted heartwarming stories of extended hands between Muslims and non-Muslims, images popped up on my feed of non-Muslim Americans going the extra distance to make Muslims feel safe here in their own hometowns, and my Muslim friends from across the country recorded moments of increased acts of warmth and kindness towards them—seemingly as though our fellow countrymen were making an effort to remind us that this was our country, too. It was as if, through Trump's outrageously hateful rhetoric, America had awoken to the reality that now was time to defend and protect a minority community that needed it. Even though Trump represented the racist underbelly of a nation, light rose to the surface, even through the most negligible of cracks, to resist it.

On September 11, 2015, I received a text message from my friend Hebah, Muslim Girl's creative director at the time, that was just as much unexpected as it was totally natural.

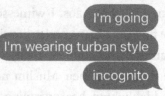

Yo should I be nervous to go to jummah

I cant tell

why

911

I'm going

I'm wearing turban style

incognito

Ya thats what im thinkin

ok i make dua for our safety

"Dua" is the Islamic term for supplication.

"Yo should I be nervous to go to *jummah*? I can't tell," it said.

Jummah is the Arabic word for Friday, the Muslim holy day of the week. In this case, she was referring to Friday prayer, our weekly religious service. We regularly attended *jummah* prayer at the Islamic Center of New York University (ICNYU) under the leadership of Imam Khalid Latif. I credit him for making it cool to be tolerant and openminded in as institutionalized of a space as the ICNYU. You can go there for any given prayer service and find devout-as-heck Muslims who never miss a religious obligation performing *salaat* alongside Muslims who smoke and drink like it's no thang whatsoever, because it isn't. That Ramadan, I wrote a Facebook status—shared by Imam Khalid, subsequently gone viral—about a white, tatted-up Muslim convert I befriended at the ICNYU one night. As I walked to the subway station with my tattooed buddy, there wasn't a piece of trash on the dirty piss-laden Fourth Street sidewalk that he wouldn't pick up and hold onto until he got to the next wastebasket to properly dispose of it, nor was there a single person in need he'd pass by without stopping to offer them *something*. To a person who didn't know any better, he didn't seem to fit the stereotypical Muslim "type" from the outside, but we all had a lot to learn from him. Islam is intended to be our great equalizer.

I had come to love the ICNYU for the space it provided, and I saw it as a home away from home—and my fellow worshipers as a second family, even though I had never personally met most of the people there. That's why, for a brief moment, I was confused, and I texted Hebah back, "Why?" I watched as the iMessage bubbles popped up. "9/11," she responded.

I almost forgot that it was the anniversary of a tragedy that became one of the worst days of our lives—a tragedy not only for the horrible terrorist act on our soil that became a symbol of our empirical resolve and the lives lost on Ground Zero, but also for the countless people still paying the collective price for an action that had nothing to do with them.

"Oh yeah, I'm wearing a turban. #incognito," I sent Hebah. For hijabis, we enjoy the privilege of being able to style our headscarves like turbans, which evoke a kind of religious ambiguity for us—they're seen as more trendy on women than religious, as they are usually expected to be worn by brown men. That's a privilege Sikh men will never enjoy. They've been just as much victimized by Islamophobia for their publicly identifiable religious garment—whether or not people can tell the religious difference. Shame. I didn't realize it until that moment that I had based my scarf style that day on the level of negative attention I would likely be subjected to in public. And it wasn't until that moment, through Hebah's texts, that I realized she had done the same—and verbalized a lived experience familiar to many Muslim women for the past decade. Our text conversation was the materialization of what goes on just beneath the surface of our everyday lives. This constant negotiation. These adaptations. The breathing, quivering epitome of the millennial generation of Muslim women. They are microdefenses, the conditioned changes we make for our safety on a day to day basis.

Another behavorial phenomenon that I've witnessed become prevalent among Muslim women is how we protect ourselves on the subway. It's almost become inscribed among Muslim women to stand further away from the edge of the platform, for fear of getting pushed onto the tracks by some rabid Islamophobe. Any New Yorker is in danger of this happening, but we, especially those of us who are veiled, are increasingly vulnerable targets of this kind of crime and so have trained ourselves to take extra precautions. In 2013, a woman killed a Hindu man by shoving him onto the tracks of an oncoming train because, as she later stated, she hated Muslims ever since 9/11 happened. Think about that. It's like the perfect perverted intersection of the typical American's ignorance of those she mindlessly hates—in this case, conflating a Hindu, or oftentimes a Sikh, with a Muslim, because, you know, brown skin—and the collective blame and incitement of violence against a people as a whole.

Another form of a microdefense that has become innate among Muslim millennials is avoiding use of the slang word *bomb*, no matter the context. It's been a really long time since I've exclaimed the common school phrase, "Man, I totally bombed that exam." This applies in public so that we don't cause any discomfort or alarm to the people around us hearing this word uttered from a Muslim mouth, as do the series of Arabic-speakers kicked off their flights after fellow passengers become suspicious of the use of their native language in such a hostile context. This also applies in private, given the invasive surveillance policies placed on Muslim communities that effectively kill our due process rights and have caused the type of language we use to come under bewildering scrutiny. In my case, I even get uneasy when my friends message me words that are on the NSA hotlist. One year, an article was published online claiming that the NSA has a list of words[4] that, when sent in electronic form, automatically prompt surveillance; one of my Muslim friends humorously Facebook chatted me

4 Dylan Love, "These Are Supposedly The Words That Make The NSA Think You're A Terrorist," *Business Insider*, June 13, 2013, http://www.businessinsider.com/nsa-prism-keywords-for-domestic-spying-2013-6.

a series of messages using those terms in all their glory. "Ha! Now I got the NSA on you!" he joked.

The youngins that we are, we have often turned to humor to help us cope with our mind-bogglingly ridiculous reality, though that doesn't negate the treacherous threat that language really pose to our lives. At the very beginning of the Summer of Hustle, I had just finished grabbing coffee with two acquaintances that worked at Al Jazeera America. We were standing outside of a Starbucks in Manhattan, discussing the internal condition of the network, which was then only creeping toward its eventual demise less than a year later. My colleagues were both Arabs— one fair-skinned woman with straight jet-black hair, the other, a dark burly man with a thick black beard. Then, there was me, rocking a *totally* inconspicuous scarf on my head. This was after I had just been told, yet again, that my start date for the program manager job for which I moved to New York was postponed, and my acquaintances were advising me to forget them and do my own thing. "Your site gets more views than our network," the producer told me. "Why would you want to work for us when you could be developing your own media company?" Good question.

As the conversation moved forward, the other woman and I noticed a blond, blue-eyed white guy hovering near us, almost eavesdropping, and acting kind of weird. Eventually, the producer said something to the effect of, "We have to hit the reset button on the entire thing," regarding Al Jazeera America's operations, and that was it. Weird White Guy abruptly interrupted us and jumped into the middle of our conversation.

"Excuse me," he said. "I'm going to be super quick and I'm just going to get right to it: When you say 'reset,' does that mean, like, starting over?" We all gave him a New York stare, super confused and highly offended at his imposition.

"Huh? What are you talking about?" we all asked.

"You said you want to hit the reset button," he continued. "Are you talking about a bomb? Are you planning to blow this place up? Are you going to kill me? I just want to know if I should call a police officer over . . ."

That was that. My colleagues both began to address him in their own assertive ways, the woman saying she'd worked for the government and was going to call a cop on *him* if he didn't walk away and stop making her feel so uncomfortable, the man giving him an intimidating death glare and demanding that he get the hell away from us. But me? I was suddenly confronted by my own suffocating vulnerability: the intense self-realization that, among the three of us, I was the only one wearing a headscarf—the only one "visibly" Muslim, that was dressed like those people on the news, and thus would be a lightning rod of attention for someone inclined to make such an outrageously racist and horrifying assumption. In seconds, I saw an imaginary series of reactive events flash before my eyes: handcuffs, NYPD ransacking my apartment, my entire life dissected and twisted, the carpet of the judicial system ripped right out from under my feet at the conceivable threat of terror. I thought of the Patriot Act, of one of my friends saying that someone he knew in college disappeared, the illegal police surveillance compound that was secretly erected on our Rutgers University campus so law enforcement could surveil our Muslim Student Association. In the age of the War on Terror, due process is no right for Muslims.

I hadn't realized the deeply subconscious reaction it would trigger in me. It was truly instinctual—the type of innate response that is ignited upon threat against one's survival—and, while my friends could afford the time to respond and challenge, my immediate need was to get as far away from him as possible. "Please, can we please leave," I begged them in a low voice between clenched teeth, so as not to panic. "Stop responding, please, let's just go." Finally, I took off, trying to put as much space between me and that individual as possible. It was so distressing that I kept looking over my shoulder, even across streets, expecting to see him following me. I was so shaken that when I finally felt that I was a safe enough distance away from him, I walked into the first café I could find and collapsed onto a wooden chair, where I would sit motionless for almost an hour.

I really don't know why that prompted such an emotional reaction out of me. Actually, I wouldn't even call it emotional—it was definitely instinctual. And I know what people would say: Well, if you're innocent, you have nothing to worry about. That's the usual response given to people who dare criticize the Patriot Act, legalizing an intrusion on our private lives across the board. But the thing is, this isn't about innocence or guilt. This is about a government with absolutely no accountability, with the legal power to do what it wants with your body simply because of your religion, which it could hold against you as an inherent threat. Bodies of color are criminalized. Black Americans can be shot dead in the seat of their cars, with a seatbelt on, for reaching for their wallets. Undocumented people can be extorted with deportation for not complying with the smallest arbitrary assertion of authority. Muslims can face the threat of torture cells and prison compounds for, I guess, making the mistake of saying the word "reset" in public. Sometimes these identities meet at one treacherous intersection.

It's moments like these that compel our microdefensiveness at the most basic level.

Entitlement can manifest itself in a variety of ways. In 2014, I was invited to speak at the C3 Summit in New York City, which regards itself as a platform dedicated to exchanging best practices and knowledge transfer between the United States and the Arab region. The event is attended by ambassadors, CEOs, and even Arab royalty, and it was the most prestigious speaking invitation I had received up to that point. I was excited to share our vision for Muslim Girl with such distinguished company. In the hours leading up to our time slot, I had been preparing my remarks in a separate room, practicing in front of my friend Hadiya, making sure my timing was perfect.

When it was time for our panel, we situated ourselves on the oversized chairs onstage and positioned our individual mics. Hadiya and my parents sat in the front row, excitedly readying their devices to record the discussion. When it was my turn to speak, I invited the audience to join me in a collective experiment that I thought would demonstrate Muslim Girl's crucial purpose. I asked everyone to whip out their phones, open up Google Image Search, type in the search term "Muslim women," and hit enter. What would they find?

After a few moments, there were gasps and guffaws emanating from around the room. Everyone fell quiet as we momentarily scrolled through the bleak search results together: a wall of dark repetitive images of faceless women hidden behind veils, sometimes with only their eyes showing, sometimes not. The media and even the information reaching us straight to our phone screens had become saturated with the same monolithic stereotypical image of Muslim women. When we deny the robust diversity of Muslim women from their representation, it's no wonder we are able to so easily smear, generalize, and sideline them.

This is where I started to open up about how Muslim Girl was born to take back to the mic, when it happened.

"Don't," interrupted a white woman sitting in the audience, on my time, with a haughty jeer. She leaned forward, releasing a sarcastic laugh. "Don't say anything to offend people."

I wanted to continue. "As I was saying—"

"I'm just saying—" she attempted to go on.

"Excuse me," I said, stopping her. "I'm the one speaking right now."

She receded—and later, during the reception, I wouldn't be able to find her to let her know how rude and offensive her action had been—but not before my friends and family gasped, astounded at Entitled White Woman's reaction. As the only veiled woman on stage, so too was I the only speaker who was interrupted at the entire summit. Even though I shut her down without a thought during the panel, I would feel remorse later that I hadn't, in the moment, demonstrated to the audience that this was the perfect example of the type of silencing by the West that Muslim women have been enduring for at least the past decade; the type of silencing that, at its core, Muslim Girl surfaced to defy.

It stunned me at the time, and it still pains and angers me to remember that moment, which became such a clear manifestation of the levels laid out by our society. Even when the veiled Muslim woman was the one on the stage, with the microphone, with the status of "speaker," a regular attendee sitting in the audience whose only role was to listen still felt entitled and superior enough to dictate what the Muslim woman would say. At the most microcosmic level, it makes it easier to see how Muslim women as a whole have been talked over, imposed upon, and told what's best for them by empire, much to their own detriment, sacrifice, and subjugation.

Similarly, at midnight on my twenty-fourth birthday, I found myself on a packed PATH train, beside one of my best friends, Shanzay. I was carrying a baby kitten in a kennel that I allowed to take up a seat next to me so that I could easily tend to him during our trip, given that the noise of his surroundings and the busy subway tracks below him left him terrified. It was an action not unlike that of the countless hipsters on the Williamsburg subways that I had witnessed treating their pets like people. As more people filed in, one woman stood quietly in front of us. Another white woman beside her with a British accent pointed at the kennel next to me and rudely said, "That's a seat." Even though it sounded like she was being unnecessarily hostile, I promptly obliged and placed the kennel on the shaky ground in front of me, to which the first woman standing in front of us politely responded with a "Thank you" before taking a seat beside us. And that was that. Or so I thought.

For some unknown reason, a white man standing beside the British woman joined in with a condescending laugh: "Yeah, that was a seat," he said to her. She joined in a self-congratulatory conversation with him, and, I guess encouraged by the new ally she made, turned back to me, gestured at the kennel, and demanded, "What's in that thing anyway?"

I, surprised that she was still pursuing an unwanted interaction with me, responded with, "I don't want to speak with you."

"Oh!" she exclaimed, turning back to the man beside her, exchanging more condescending looks of contempt. "How rude!" she said to the man, to his agreement.

"No, she just doesn't want to talk to you," Shanzay interjected. "She removed the kennel and said she doesn't want to speak with you, so why do you insist on continuing a conversation with her?"

"Yes, wow, so abrasive. All you did was want to start a conversation," the man conferred with the woman. Their disgust really came from the rejection of their feeling of entitlement to my time and attention, as if, when spoken to, I was mandated to respond. If it's difficult to grasp the concept, then consider women's anger around the phenomenon of men feeling entitled to tell a woman to *smile* at them, asserting their feeling of entitlement and authority over her behavior in the public space, as if she must always appear pleasant and cheerful to their liking. No, I don't have to respond to you when spoken to.

You may have also noticed the selective memory of the man's quick response of calling me "abrasive"—a personification of women of color who are angry (and rightfully so) who are historically characterized as being barbarically dispossessed of themselves and seized by emotion. It's rooted in colonial suppression of colonized subjects—that denunciation of resistance to occupiers as unprompted hostility rather than an assertion of autonomy. In this case, this man conveniently forgot who was the instigator. Upon initial interaction, I responded cordially; but the woman insisted that she was entitled to more from me. The man eagerly agreed with the woman as if my "abrasive" response—simply not engaging her—was not prompted by her contemptible intrusion in the first place.

These everyday interactions are leaking remnants of our colonial history, and the way we interact with and view minorities in our society as being outsiders that are less-than. Consider the ways in which this is playing out on a national level in our politics today. For example, the #BlackLivesMatter movement has been painted by corporate media as being uncivil, violent, destructive, and unwarranted, as if the bodies of black boys that cops have shot dead in the streets, or the very unequal framework of power administering so-called justice in the first place, had nothing to do with rousing the people to action.

The same can be said of the occupation of Palestine, in which a people, stripped of their land, property, defenses, and resources, are constantly goaded by colonial settlements, arbitrary use of force, and international law violations. When they are roused to react against their occupiers, they are then painted both by their occupier, its allies, and Western media as hoodless terrorists. They further paint the occupier as having done nothing more than simply "exist." This is then used to justify further violence inflicted upon the occupied to assert control, subjugation, and superiority. Take it and shut up. Speak only when spoken to.

The woman and man on the train continued to engage in a conversation with each other, exceptionally loud within earshot—that immature *Mean Girls*-esque thing you do in high school when you want someone to hear and know that you're talking about them without actually engaging them. The woman was a transplant from London for a job here in New York, much to the delight of her newfound companion. I couldn't help myself and we needed a laugh; I turned to Shanzay:

"These damn immigrants! They come to *our* country to take *our* jobs and then try to tell us how to live . . ."

It's so easy to regard moments like these as exceptions, but really they are just manifestations of a long history of Western attitudes toward people of color. I see it in the same way as a white male presidential candidate vilifying minorities and immigrants in our country, when he doesn't necessarily belong here himself. In the case of Donald Trump, his grandparents immigrated here from Germany in 1885.[5] Meanwhile, Muslims first arrived to the shores of America at least several generations prior, possibly encountering Native American tribes even before making up 10 to 15 percent of slaves brought from Africa.[6] As a testament to the power of racism, this isn't enough to stop Trump from audaciously making the claim that Muslims do not deserve to be a part of this country, as if he has more right to this space, this land, than we do, the authority to dictate our right to it, and, by extension, assert that we do not belong here. Given their history of subjugation and the fact that our black brothers and sisters literally built this country, Muslims bear the real entitlement to tell Trump to get the hell out of our country.

5 Alexander Dluzak, "Donald Trump's German Roots," DW.com, February 29, 2016, http://www.dw.com/en/donald-trumps-german-roots/a-19015570.
6 "Islam in America," PBS, http://www.pbs.org/opb/historydetectives/feature/islam-in-america/.

Epilogue

I was sitting beside a representative from UN Women at a closed-meeting roundtable at the United Nations, discussing the needs of faith-based feminist organizations, when one of my former college professors walked in. She was a famous white feminist leader in the women's movement whose lessons—the ability to learn from her directly—were coveted as an honor by our competitive class of women's leadership certification candidates. She spoke gently with a keen grasp of the issues we were facing on a global scale, putting them into accessible context for us in our often far-removed lecture room on Rutgers's Douglass campus in New Brunswick, New Jersey.

That year, I barely made it to a single lecture of hers on time. I was exerting all my energy and attention on putting into practice my higher education outside of the classroom. I constantly skipped classes to attend events in New York City that would bring me, in some semblance, closer to actualizing my dreams. I remember leaving campus to attend a media class at the United Nations, only to meet Tawakkol Karman, a Libyan revolutionary and the first Arab woman to be a Nobel Peace Prize laureate, leading a demonstration outside of its headquarters. I don't remember what the content of the class was that I had to make up, but I still have that photo with Tawakkol of our smiling faces, mine beaming a little more excitedly in our half-hug.

My fellow women's leadership scholars turned my attendance

into an inside joke, and by the end of the semester, my feminist professor took such great offense to it that she rightfully reported me to our program director. "Do you understand how much of a privilege it is to learn from this teacher?" the director asked me in her office during a scheduled meeting. "She's giving her time to teach you and you show up to her lectures late or not at all."

It's been two years since I graduated from that program at Rutgers, and now I am part of a coalition with that same feminist professor to decide on a resolution to present to the Commission on the Status of Women. She walked past the conference table, taking the seat right across from me. Then she looked up, saw my eager smile and excited wave, and grinned right back at me. Batons being passed.

As the youngest person in the room, it's impossible to think that I would have found myself in the same space as her had I not been making those sacrifices to cut classes and hone my interests in real life, but it begs the question of why I had to make those sacrifices in the first place. For women of color, "leaning in" doesn't always work. Sometimes you need to jump over a wall, break through a window, and kick down a door to force your way in. Sometimes you need to do this even—and especially—when the gatekeepers fail to see your worth as clearly as you do.

At the same time, it was having the privilege of learning from that feminist professor and a long line of educators and mentors— from Jordan to college, from protests to media—that led me to this room.

The last time I attended the Commission on the Status of Women, it was with my fellow women's leadership scholars during that certification program, and we would commute from New Jersey to the United Nations together. On one of the nights following a commission assembly, my friend Katie and I were walking to Port Authority, heading home to Jersey, when we decided to extend our trip in the city and visit the Empire State Building.

"Can you look up the directions, please?" I asked her, years before I could repeat the subway stops in my sleep.

"Why can't you do it?" she asked.

"I'm a Muslim, I can't have that in my phone. Looking up directions to the Empire State Building? God knows what people could think." The microdefense had become so second nature, such a preconditioned way of thinking, and the explanation fell out of my mouth so unconsciously that I didn't think anything of it until Katie furrowed her brow at me.

"Wow. That's really sad that you have to think that way. It's sad that it's even a thought that has to cross your mind." That's probably when I realized how strange it was.

About a year after college graduation, right at the start of what would become the Summer of Hustle, I was getting coffee with another one of our program's women's leadership alumni, Arabelle Sicardi, in a hipster Bushwick coffee shop with wooden tables and cheap Wi-Fi. She had just resurfaced from a media whirlwind surrounding her controversial resignation from BuzzFeed after they censored her social criticism of a major beauty corporation that was one of their advertisers. Arabelle is a half-Taiwanese, half-white beauty blogger who writes about the intersection between beauty, race, and society.

I had just made the fateful decision to leave Al Jazeera America behind and cast my dreams into the New York winds like a kite to see what they would return. I was reacquainting myself with Brooklyn, living off my savings, and wondering just how I was going to do this.

"You can do this," Arabelle encouraged me. "This is what you were meant to do."

It would be at a subway station of the beloved L train that I'd pick up a call from a *Teen Vogue* editor, Arabelle's boss. Arabelle was fulfilling her childhood dreams of penning a beauty column for them, and she referred to the editor as her squad when she introduced us. She told him he had to hear about the amazing work we were doing for women's voices.

By the end of the summer we had worked on a feature with *Teen Vogue* that would herald a breakthrough in Muslim women's visibility in the media. The feature, proclaiming our voices as Muslim women "titanic," would usher in a whole new caliber of coverage and representation of our issues, voices, and activities in the mainstream. It would be the first of a series of great works we would do with them that year, the first of their kind with any major American magazine. By the end of the year, I would be flying to Los Angeles for a photoshoot at *Teen Vogue*'s studios for their "New Faces of Feminism" cover story in the February 2016 print issue. It would be the first time that a veiled Muslim woman would be featured in a main spread—for a celebratory topic completely unrelated to Islam, the Middle East, or terrorism, no less. I became a new face for feminism, and I just so happened to be a veiled Muslim woman.

One of the questions I am asked the most is "What motivates you?" It's always been a difficult one to answer. It's less about motivation and more about survival. It's not our choice to stay motivated when the alternative is hate crimes, wars, and more walls. In the United States alone, Muslims are only one hate crime away from life or death. International images of women and children being targeted and families being ripped apart by the war on terror, with more and more policies disproportionately impacting communities of color, are not our privileged motivations. Allowing another generation of little girls to grow up being told they don't belong, that their bodies are less valuable, less human, is simply not an option.

I dreamed I had a daughter. I could see the back of her reading over a book, but I could never see her face. She was hidden behind long, dark hair and was very quiet, receding to the shadows of a room but still glowing beneath my sheer admiration of her. She was so beautiful, and in my dream I knew that hers was a beauty that the world would seek to destroy because it would not be able to understand it. I was seized by the innate, instinctive nature of a mother compelled to protect. I felt this desperate urge to protect her from the world, shield her from the cruelty that I knew would inevitably befall her and to which she did not deserve to be subjected. I woke up, my heart still pounding with this raw emotion. She stayed on my mind for days until I spoke to an intuitive friend who told me that the little girl in my dream was me, and that protection was what I had wanted most when I was the little girl's age.

I think of that little girl every single day. I thought of her when I was tagged in an Instagram photo of a teenage girl ripping the glossy page of me out of her *Teen Vogue* issue to hang on her bedroom walls, much like I did with the pages of waify white models from the magazines I read in junior high. I thought of her at the United State of Women Summit, when a Muslim mother recognized me and ran up to me with her little four-year-old daughter, asking if she could introduce us because she wanted to show her daughter that she could be anything she wanted. I thought of her, especially, when a Hindu mother approached me to tell me that she prints out MuslimGirl.com articles to read with her fourteen-year-old daughter before bed as their self-esteem-building exercise at the end of a long day. I thought of how two years earlier, I almost stopped myself from going to my media internship, the image ringing in my head of a Hindu man getting pushed onto subway tracks as retribution for 9/11.

I think of the little girls we were and the little girls we could have been, and the little girls who never were and what little girls will be if we have anything to say about it. I think of how our generation is a fateful one. We were the little girls who had our voices robbed of us. We were the little girls who had our bodies and our homelands ripped apart while our hands were tied behind our backs. We were the little girls who were told to sit down and shut up while our world betrayed us. We are rising up—we are the ones reclaiming our voices, the ones talking back, and the ones reminding the world that no, we haven't forgotten. We grew to become our own saviors.

Afterword

I'm twenty-five years old now and five months into Trump's America.

Ten days after his January 20 inauguration to the presidency, Trump made good on his campaign promise and brought eighteen months of hateful, anti-Muslim rhetoric to a climax: he instituted the Muslim Ban.

It's funny because since writing this book, the most common question I've received from naysayers and even (shocking!) some people in the media has been, "Why are you wasting your time talking about Islamophobia in the West when you should be talking about violence against Muslim women in Muslim countries?"

If there's anything I hope this book and the crap show that has been our international politics demonstrates, it's that anti-Muslim bigotry and worldwide violence against Muslim women are intertwined. It starts with something as seemingly inconsequential as the way we use the word "terrorism." Here are the CliffsNotes: it's only ever talked about when Muslims are committing it. Then we use this label to classify all Muslims into one giant, different group, an "Other" that doesn't belong, even if they're a born-and-raised Jersey girl like me. Once we've normalized that sentiment, it becomes common for people to hurl insults like "You people don't belong here! Go back to your country!" Then you get this: a white supremacist in Portland, Oregon, harassing two Muslim women on the metro. When three non-Muslim men stepped in to defend them, the man slashed their necks, killing two of them and hospitalizing the third. Or you get this: a veiled seventeen-year-old girl leaving her mosque in Virginia one Ramadan night, only to be targeted by a man who kidnapped, raped, and beat her to death with a baseball bat before throwing her body into a pond—which still no one called a hate crime.

On a national level, that's how something like a Muslim ban happens; on an international level, it's the destructive and civilian-ridden War on Terror, yet when we look back at historic tragedies like internment camps, we click our tongues and shake our heads, self-assuredly asking ourselves, "How could humanity let it happen?"

Of course, the anger spreads. The global wave of anti-Muslim sentiment over the past year has been astounding: France elected to ban Muslim women from choosing to cover themselves on beaches, which the media painted with one broad stroke as the burqini ban. Angela Merkel was ironically heralded as a feminist icon for not wearing a headscarf on a visit to Saudi Arabia, while rallying to deny Muslim women of that same freedom of choice to veil in Germany. And the European Union has ruled to allow employers to ban the headscarf in workplaces. A part of me wants to laugh at how silly it is for the world to get riled up over this piece of fabric on my head. But of course the rest of me recognizes this for what it is: the continuing, evolving attack on who we are because of our religious beliefs.

Isn't that what we're accusing the terrorists of?

But the adversity of these past months has also been breathing new life into resistance, as adversity often does. This year, we witnessed one of the largest global protests in history for women—a protest co-led by a Muslim woman. We saw the first veiled American Muslim woman compete in the Olympics—and win. A Muslim woman basketball player denied the opportunity to compete professionally in hijab championed policy changes that would drop the ban. The first veiled Muslim woman graced a *Vogue* cover. And most of these women just so happen to be black, too.

And, in the first one hundred days of Trump's presidency, MuslimGirl.com launched the first global Muslim Women's Day campaign, which dominated the Internet and flooded everyone's timelines and newsfeeds with an unprecedented level of positive, diverse, and new representation of Muslim women in online media. Silenced who?

If there's one lesson we can learn from Muslim women in today's political climate, it's that nobody is voiceless. There are just those who are systematically silenced. For many marginalized communities, that silencing is largely rooted in racism, ignorance, and supreme exceptionalism. But there is another underlying reason: it's the festering fear of the powerful and seismic shift that could happen to the world if those voices speak and are heard. Our resistance is rooted in the immovable belief that we deserve this—that we owe it to ourselves and to each other to find the strength, courage, and resolve to speak our truths.

And those who stand in our way? We'll leave them behind on the wrong side of history, so that when future generations look back on us, they won't be asking, "How could they?"

They'll be saying, "They did."

Acknowledgments

Rabbina laka al hamdu wal shukr,
hamdan wa shukran katheeran,
tayebban mubarakan,
kaman yanbayaghi bejelaly wajheka
wa atheemy soltaneka.

We are all made of star stuff, and I've been made up of my fair share of stars. It is impossible to name every incredible soul who has brought this book to life, the many friends, family, allies, and supporters that have been its lifeblood, and everyone along the way who has added their touch to this historic journey. All I can say is, from the bottom of my heart, thank you for bringing us to this moment.

Salam Baba, thanks for being my biggest motivator, my rock, and the one constant in my life. None of this would have happened if it weren't for you. Mama, you are my soul, and I hope you never forget that everything I am is you. Faris and Ameer, thank you for putting up with me and being the two guys I can always count on. I hope it's been worth it. This book is courtesy of Ameer's 3 a.m. Dunkin runs.

To the #MuslimGirlArmy—every editor, writer, reader, and supporter we ever had along the way—I am who I am because of you. Clique, thank you for sitting with me. I love you like air. Thank you to our tribe, those who enthusiastically backed our

Acknowledgments

work, for giving their vote of confidence to the girls in diners. It is the honor of my life to work with you all. Thank you to the league of superwomen who make up my many mentors—we stand on the shoulders of giants and our work is another link in the chain.

Arabelle Sicardi, you are my fairy godmother; thank you for being the definition of a powerful ally. Abdul Rehman Khan and Sabah Abbasi, thank you for being my sounding board whenever I needed one. Special thanks to Jenna Masoud for snapping the photo that landed in a thousand interviews.

I want to express deep gratitude to the team that made my childhood dream of writing a book come true. Thank you to my agent, Erin Malone, for guiding me through the process of publishing my first book and translating a whole new world for me. Thank you especially to my editor, Ebony LaDelle, for sharing in my vision for this book and truly bringing it to life, and to Jonathan Karp for the opportunity of chronicling a crucial experience during this historic moment. Thank you to Maureen Cole, Ashfia Alam, Richard Rhorer, and Jackie Seow for all the work you put into making this endeavor a success. Thank you Zareen Jaffery for being a guiding light for Muslim bookworms.

Most importantly, thank you to everyone who has been part of the ride.